To my mother, Beverly, whose love and protection of all animals inspired wonder and imagination in her young son.

SEEN ANYTHING GOOD?

Seasons of Birds in Midcoast Maine

by Don Reimer

Seen Anything Good?
Copyright © 2020 Don Reimer

ISBN: 978-1-63381-234-5

All rights reserved. No part of this book may be reproduced in any form or by any electronic or mechanical means, including information storage and retrieval systems, without permission in writing from the author, except by a reviewer, who may quote brief passages in review.

Designed and produced by:
Maine Authors Publishing
12 High Street, Thomaston, Maine
www.maineauthorspublishing.com

Printed in the United States of America

Contents

Introduction 1
Seen Anything Good? 3

Part I: Spring Is in the Air

A Bluebird Day 7
All for Science 9
April Waterfowl 11
Backyard Wren 15
Birding by Ear 17
Celebrating the River 19
Chestnut on the Sides 21
Connecting People with Birds 23
Eyes on the River 25
Gnatcatcher 28
Ravens' Grove 30
Roadkills 33
Ruff Around the Edges 36
Safe and Sound 39
Sherm's Worms 42
Wet Weather Birding 44
Woodcock! 46

Part II: Summer Sightings

A Nesting Report Card 51
Antics 53

Banded Birds 55
Chasing Loons 58
From Russia with Love 61
Good for the Heart. 63
Heading Offshore 65
Hiding in the Woods. 68
Maine's Fish Crows. 71
MEGU Equals Mew Gull 73
Venturing for Vultures. 76
Summering with Vultures 79
Two Grouse. 85
Voices from the Woods 87
Exploring the Rockland Bog 90
Weskeag Sparrows 92
What's a Piscivore?. 95
Whip-poor-wills 97

Part III: Moving into Fall

A Visit from Big Bird 101
Bronzed Cowbird 103
Déjà Vu 106
Dovekie in the River 109
Fallouts 111
Lost and Found. 114
Raptor Migration. 116
September Shorebirds .119
The Air They Breathe .122
The Larger Waders. 124
Tooty Fruity. 126
Turkey Tales 128
Wedding Doves. 131

Part IV: Our Coastal Winters

An Old Red Notebook 135
Are Birds Important? 138
Caching For Winter 140
City Falcons 142
Coping with Winter 144
Gallinule 146
Inchworms 148
January Coots 150
Just Ducky 152
Kids and Eagles 155
NIMBYs 158
Owl Moon 160
Raven on a Mission 163
Stakeouts 166
A 2014 Snow Job 169

Part V: For Birders' Eyes Only

Birds and Kids 173
Birds of a Different Feather 175
Caps and Such 177
Dump Picking 179
Just Ask Alexa 181
Making a List; Checking It Twice 183
Loon in a Bathtub 185
Mad About Decoys 187
Page-Turner 190
Personal Ads 192
Perspectives 194
Photographing That Bird 196

Scarce as Hen's Teeth. 199
Skepticisms 201
Going to the Movies 203
E is for Egg 205
Through the Eyes of Birds. 208
Yearbooks. 210
Your Own Birding Patch 212

Part VI: Some People Worth Knowing

My Friend Mark 217
Tom Martin and Monhegan Island. 220

About the Author 223

Introduction

Although I couldn't specify a date, an abiding interest in birds was clearly rooted in my early adolescence. Maybe it was the irrepressible fascination with the yellow pet canary caged in my grandmother's living room. Or it might have been later sojourns into the Russells' henhouse, located across the roadway from my childhood home in New Harbor. The Russells' cackling Rhode Island Reds became my learning station for observing social structure and behavior among birds. When hens occasionally graduated toward stewpot status, I got firsthand experience in avian anatomy and physiology, as Mrs. Russell dunked the feathered carcasses inside wide buckets of scalding water to pluck and dress them for cooking. Details of the hens' inner workings also enthralled me. Noting the seminal, strings of planet-like orange yolks awaiting fruition inside the hen's ovary casings was a revelation that stuck in my mind.

A second phase of awareness involved the wild birds seen at our home feeding stations. In the mid-1950s, feeding birds was far less of a phenomenon than it has become today. A few townspeople maintained basic feeders, though, and just outside our kitchen window, my mom positioned a pole-mounted platform containing sunflower seeds and occasional bread scraps scattered on the ground. For us, this convenient arrangement meant reliable, intimate access to the chickadees, goldfinches, and sparrows that became our welcome guests. During years of winter finch irruptions, chitty mobs of pine siskins and common redpolls would magically appear. In fortunate winters, groups of sleek Bohemian waxwings and evening grosbeaks spent time around the yard. Patterned in their bright yellow tones, with crisp black markings more suggestive of tropical climes, the thick-billed grosbeaks brought clambering excitement to the neighborhood.

The number of birders, or *bird-watchers* as they were termed in those same decades, was limited along the coast. A recollection of seeing two birders probing through roadside shrubbery at Pemaquid Point comes to mind. I was intrigued by the binoculars around their necks and the purposeful manner of their quest. The pair stood riveted on some obscured bird, seemingly oblivious to the cars slowly driving past, a few feet away. With great envy, I pondered what they might be seeing. I'd already come to understand that bird-watchers were an eccentric bunch and, perhaps, even a bit ditzy. But whether bird-watching implied eccentricity or ditziness, it didn't matter to me. I was eager to sign on.

Through my persistent study and observation, birds became a touchstone in my later life. I paid them special notice at every opportunity and in every conceivable setting. In adulthood, I would even pursue some of them from a vastly different perspective, as game birds.

In 2007, I posed a question to *Rockland Free Press* editor Alice McFadden: Did she think a column on birds would be of interest to her readers? "Yes," she answered, "let's give it a try." I'd also begun taking bird photos through my spotting scope, a process, then-relatively new, known as *digiscoping*. Although those early photos were limited to stationary birds, I managed to include at least one bird-related photo with each of my columns. Eventually, I purchased a legitimate, high-speed digital camera, capable of capturing distant birds in flight.

Like a fleeting bird, the years have flown by. I've written dozens of newspaper articles that were generally well received and commented upon by readers. Never intending to write a book at all, I was persuaded to publish some of my writings in book form by the encouraging comments and prompts from readers. My original premise was to bring forth clear and straightforward information, while developing appreciation of birds among the general public and, perhaps, spur an interest in adopting practical conservation measures. I hope I've accomplished some of those goals.

Seen Anything Good?

On encountering fellow birders in the field, a queried expression is commonly heard: "Seen anything good?" That, of course, depends on our expectations for the day, and our personal definitions of what constitutes a *"good" bird*. Blue jays are common enough here in Maine, but would be a hotline bird in California. An oriole sighted during Maine's midwinter months might be termed a *good bird,* because of the odd-seasonal timing. Any species previously unseen or totally unknown to us could automatically rate a *good bird* status.

Often we use the term *rare* to describe birds that appear outside of their normal ranges. But rarity is a relative concept that can change with time. Eighty years ago, turkey vultures were considered rare in Maine. According to Ralph Palmer's *Maine Birds,* vultures were listed as "rare visitors, mostly in coastal counties" up through the era of the 1930s. Currently, statewide distribution of vultures has altered their status to a considerable extent. Now relegated to a common status, are nesting vultures still valued as *good birds* in Maine?

Consider John James Audubon, who was discovering and naming previously unknown species of birds in the early 1800s. Some species, like the flock of passenger pigeons that darkened the skies during migration periods, were commonplace and apparently undervalued then. In 1836, Audubon proclaimed the passenger pigeon as the most abundant songbird in America. One hundred years later the species was extinct. For Audubon, a species like the chestnut-sided warbler was rare during his lifetime. Today this prolific warbler thrives in our eastern woodlands. Still a *good bird*?

Over thirty years ago, I observed a male European goldfinch in company with a flock of American goldfinches at a West Rockport feeder. This was a gorgeous, multi-colored finch with a bright red face and throat. The species was introduced into New Jersey from Europe in the early 1900s, but had limited breeding success there. Later attempts at introduction occurred in Massachusetts and the Mid-west. Some of these birds were also kept in captivity. Since surviving wild populations of the finch were thought to be extinct at the time of my West Rockport sighting, its provenance remained unresolved. To my way of thinking, it was still a *very good bird* to see.

PART I

Spring Is in the Air!

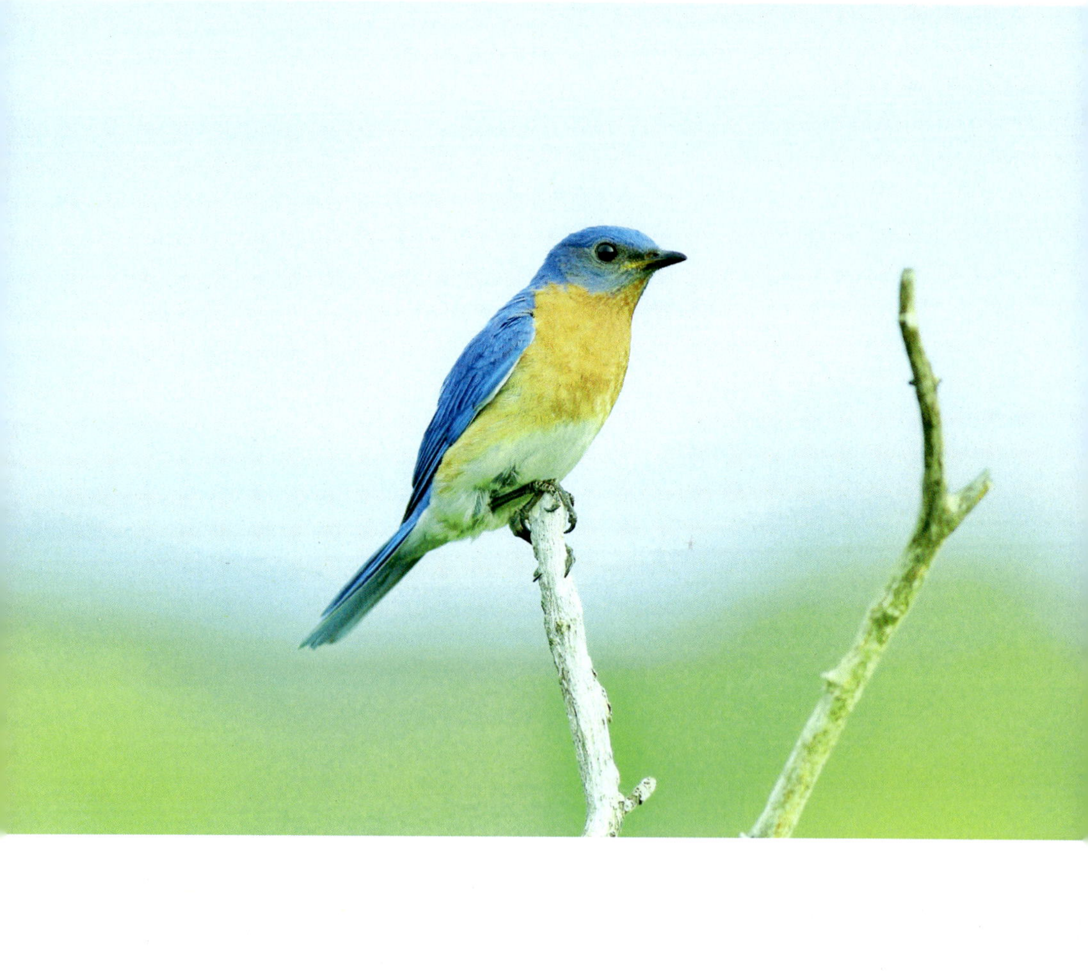

A Bluebird Day

We've heard the old expression "a bluebird day." When I researched its true origins, I discovered it's quite unrelated to actual bluebirds. The term apparently came from downhill skiers in describing a perfectly sunny, beautiful day following an overnight deposit of powdery snow. Go figure.

Found in open woodlands, farmlands, orchards, and occasional suburban settings, eastern bluebirds are small, compact members of the thrush family with rusty throats and white belly. The depth of the male's brilliant, royal blue coloration fluctuates with changes in ambient light conditions. Females are more grayish above with bluish tinges to wings and tail.

Eastern bluebirds prefer open areas surrounded by trees that offer suitable nesting cavities. Through the mid 1900s, bluebirds were a familiar component of orchards and farm sites, but populations declined to almost near-extinction levels by the 1960s. Following a proliferation of nest-box projects and so-called *bluebird trails*, bluebirds are once again common sights along roadways, field edges, golf courses, and other open habitats. Bluebirds begin seeking out nesting sites by mid-March in the north. Breeding activity lasts from early May through August, with most laying females producing two to three broods per year. After broods have fledged, it is important to remove old nesting materials and scrub the box with a 10 percent bleach solution.

Nearly two-thirds of the bluebird diet consists of insects and other invertebrates, helping people to control hordes of insect pests. Their mainstay diets include quantities of grasshoppers, crickets, and beetles. Earthworms, spiders, millipedes, centipedes, sow bugs, and snails also supplement their protein needs. To lure bluebirds to your yard, it is suggested you add crunched-up peanuts or dried mealworms to your feeders, at about four feet off the ground.

In years of relatively mild weather, the late fall is a favorable time to spot groups of bluebirds massed along power lines or fencing. Bluebirds form social congregations in fall that may number fifty to one hundred birds in appropriate habitats. Around the midcoast region, they are often found in open terrains, such as the farmlands near Clarry Hill in Union, Beech Hill in Rockport, and along the notches of Appleton Ridge.

The species' winter diet consists mainly of wild fruits and berries. Some preferred winter foods include dogwood, hawthorn, wild grape, bayberries, and barberry. The velvety fruit clusters of staghorn sumac make an accessible snack that is often consumed in the late winter season, after preferred wild foods are depleted.

Two other hardy thrush species, American robin and, occasionally, hermit thrush, can tolerate our northeastern winters. Reliable winter food supplies and snow depth are steering factors in whether they remain or venture farther south.

All for Science

We nature lovers are curious folks who pursue the inside scoop on wild creatures of all kinds. Case in point: While birding in late February 2017, John Weinrich and I encountered a large alder thicket, blanketed with grayish-white cocoons. This interesting spectacle piqued our citizen-scientific instincts, so we each brought home a cocoon sample for extended observation and follow-up. John secured his science experiment to a bush outside his home. I placed mine inside a ceramic mug that housed a dozen or so ballpoint pens on my computer desk.

By March 11, I noticed some wriggling motions amid the stack of ballpoint pens, where troops of fuzzy caterpillars now freely roamed. Yikes, my science experiment had hatched! Yikes again: these appeared to be brown-tailed moth caterpillars that can produce toxic, itchy effects on human skin! For the record, John's outdoor subjects remained latent into late April. Despite our misguided science adventures, what had we gained through these comparative efforts? Possibly some insights about timing variations of insect hatches in future years, in the face of progressive climate change? For now, I'll stick with that somewhat plausible rationale.

The Spring of 2018 offered a new, and far safer, opportunity for birders to participate in meaningful citizen-science as birds arrive for the Maine nesting season: the Maine Bird Atlas Project, a five-year study designed to identify all bird species that breed within the state, and learn more about their numbers and distribution. Maine conducted its first breeding bird atlas between 1978 and 1983. Resting on the thirty-seven-year-old findings from the previous atlas study, our current understanding of bird diversity and distribution across the state is significantly dated.

Through the Maine Bird Atlas Project, hundreds of citizen volunteers adopted survey blocks or made incidental observations near their homes or camps or during their travels throughout Maine. It was a great chance for bird-lovers to become true citizen scientists.

April Waterfowl

April is an active month for waterfowl movements throughout the Northeast, as migrant flocks of Canada geese and ducks push northward. Given their narrow, pointed wing structures, soaring flight is not an option for waterfowl. They must use powered flight in their trans-regional movements. Responding to migratory urges triggered by lengthening *photoperiods*, many groups of birds are hard-wired for migration. The term photoperiod refers to the relative lengths of day and night during a twenty-four-hour period.

Skeins of waterfowl funnel northward along thermodynamic temperature gradients called *isotherms*. These latitudinal points on a map represent connecting lines of earth surface that share the same temperature at a given time, or the same mean temperature for a given period. For Canada geese, an isothermal value of 35°F (16°C) appears to be a prime influencer on northward progress. Geese advancing beyond the springtime freeze zones could face limited food and frozen-water conditions.

Migrating waterfowl travel at speeds of twenty-five to fifty miles per hour; their altitude varies, based on the particular species and their intended destinations. Near to shore, most migrants fly within one hundred to two hundred feet of the water. Birds such as scoters and eiders frequently fly within feet of the water surface, taking advantage of ground effect. Ground effect helps generate lift and reduces drag, as downward wing forces react against water surfaces. By contrast, during longer-distance land journeys, high-flying waterfowl may appear as mere distant specks on the horizon.

Demonstrating social cohesiveness, waterfowl often migrate in groups and nest in colonial settings. Flocks assume varied configurations that serve several navigational purposes. Scoters and eiders fly in straight lines. Flocks of geese and cormorant fly in shifting formations that provide aerodynamic benefits to individual flock members in expending less physical energy and effort, while improving flight speeds. In theory, the collective "compass bearings" of individual members contribute to improved navigation for the flock.

By spring, waterfowl have reached peak breeding plumages. Pairs of overwintering long-tailed ducks remain along our coastlines through April, when they shift toward tundra nesting grounds. The drake long-tail's distinguishing, whip-like tail and draping scapular (shoulder) feathers make him easy to recognize. His loud, ringing "ow-ow-oodle-ow" calls transmit readily over the water as well.

The largest of the three merganser species, common mergansers nest in hollow trees in parts of northern Maine and Canada. By April, the green-headed drakes have begun spring courtship rituals, raising their spear-shaped tails and performing head-bobs to attract a mate. Males give hoarse croaks when alarmed, and twanging calls during courtship.

American wigeons pass through Maine each spring on their return to remote Canadian nesting areas. Smaller than mallards, this splendid dabbling duck features a smallish, silver-gray bill with black tip. Formerly known as *baldpate*, the male's white forehead distinguishes it from other surface-feeding ducks.

In the Midcoast Maine region, Weskeag Marsh and Chickawaukee Lake offer first-rate spring viewing opportunities. Further south, sections of Merrymeeting Bay on the Kennebec River are well worth a visit, and the ice-out period at Sabattus Pond is another smart bet for spring waterfowl.

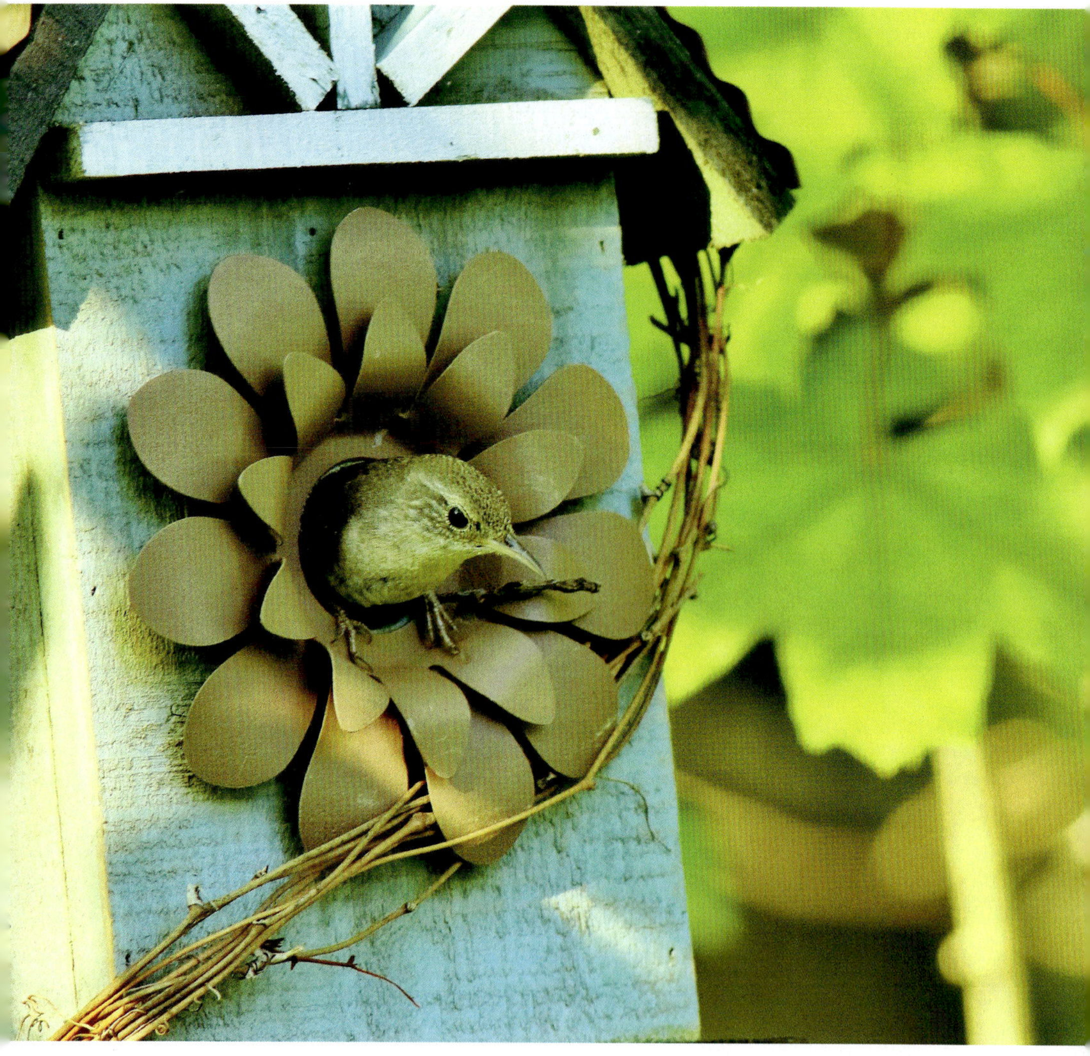

Backyard Wren

For several spring weeks, a diminutive brown bird has sung energetically in my backyard. His jumbled notes are interspersed with scolding chatters, and his trilled song is forceful and persistent. It's a male house wren working at peak energy to secure a mate. Females will sing a bit too, mainly to answer their mates shortly after pairing. In keeping with their bold vocal tendencies, house wrens can sometimes be coaxed into view with mouth squeaks and spishing sounds made by humans. Ranging between parts of Canada and into South America, house wrens are the most widely distributed bird in the Americas, and the single-most common wren species.

House wrens nest in a variety of cavity settings, from woodpecker holes to manufactured nesting boxes. Occasionally, these creative little mites will utilize an outdoor flower pot or a drainpipe. Three apparent nesting options are available in my backyard, all manufactured nest structures. As wrens will commonly do, my backyard wren has crammed each nest box full of small sticks. Wrens are the epitome of over-achievers, crafting several "dummy" nests within their territory. Next, the foundation of twigs is topped with soft nesting materials, such as grasses and hair. The female wren will make the final nest selection. Being highly competitive individuals, house wrens are known to pierce eggs of neighboring wrens and other birds within their perceived territory.

Another wren species that may nest near to people is the Carolina wren. Whereas the house wren's generally brown and gray plumage lacks true flair, the slightly larger Carolina wren has some standout physical attributes. Males and females share identical rusty backsides, buffy cinnamon underparts, and a prominent white eye-stripe.

While Carolina wrens nest throughout southern and central Maine, the northern edge of the species' Maine breeding range fluctuates, depending on the severity of a given winter season. Remaining together throughout the year, Carolina wrens favor open woods with thickets, brush piles, and tangles. Their primary diet is insects, but Carolinas will consume fruits and berries during the colder months. And if you happen to hear a rhythmic, frolicking "teakettle, teakettle" song issuing from brushy cover, you are in the company of a Carolina wren.

Not all wrens are restricted to dry land habitats. Marsh wrens prefer wetland areas of cattails, sedges, bulrushes, and tall stands of phragmites. Beyond fresh water habitats, marsh wrens are found in cordgrass salt marshes such as Weskeag Marsh in South Thomaston, where I find them in summer. Marsh wrens often hold their tail in a cocked, upright position as they splay their bodies between stalks of vertical vegetation. This industrious species is possibly the champion of nest building acumen, fashioning twenty or more nests during one season!

Hearing his rapid, buzzy trills amid the lush green stands of cordgrasses, I edged forward for a closer look. Eventually the male wren popped up to render full-throated song from the grass tops. To our untrained human ear, the wren's vocal renditions may sound simple and perhaps redundant. In fact, this species has an impressive gallery of fifty to two hundred song types. Nightfall doesn't silence these wrens either, since they may continue to sing through the night. Neighboring males engage in complex, counter-sung duels in their individual bids for nesting success.

And what about that expectant male house wren in my backyard? Unsuccessful at attracting a mate, he's apparently moved on now. That's nature for you.

Birding by Ear

This matter begins at the office of a Middletown, Connecticut, audiologist one late March. John, a former high school chum, had invited me to attend the annual conference of the Connecticut Ornithological Association, and later do some weekend birding at nearby Hammonasset Beach.

As part of the general aging process, some older individuals experience gradual hearing loss, particularly in the higher sound registers. John's two new hearing aids had helped some in the recent month, but he lacked total satisfaction in certain ways—he could not detect the high-pitched, squeaky-wheel song of a black and white warbler. John's hearing aids needed further evaluation and adjustment, and I'd thought of a possible resolution to his protracted issue.

Shortly after John entered the examining room, the audiologist motioned me inside. I placed my iPod, containing the songs of six hundred North American birds, on a table six feet from John. Dialing up the black and white warbler vocalization, I pressed the play button: "wheeza, wheeza, wheeza." John couldn't detect a single note.

"Not to worry," replied the audiologist as he rubbed his palms together with mounting confidence, "I love a challenge!" The audiologist connected John's two hearing aids to a sound analysis computer system, and boosted the high-pitch capacity on both devices. Following some minor adjustments and a final tweaking, John smiled, saying: "I can hear the warbler!"

On returning to Maine, we were experiencing the preliminary stages of April's morning bird song. American robins, house finches, goldfinches, cardinals, song sparrows, eastern phoebes, red-winged blackbirds, and the woodpecker clans were starting to vocalize. These were species that wintered locally or principally somewhere within the continental U.S.

By early to mid-May, waves of incoming neo-tropical migrants erupt in complex soundscapes, as the true dawn choruses of spring commence. In areas of varied habitat, it is possible to hear a dozen or more species singing simultaneously. Those exceptional spring mornings are like Tower of Babel experiences, where each individual species announces its presence and stakes territorial claims with specific song and dialect.

Even for seasoned birders, it can take years to learn well all the songs of Maine's roughly 230 nesting species. With the warbler songs in particular, the all-too-brief singing season affords limited opportunities to wholly master the task.

In broadest auditory terms, birds that nest in thicker, heavy cover have lower-pitched voices that carry farther and punch through tangled habitats. The ovenbird, a ground-nesting warbler, airs a loud "TEACHER, TEACHER, TEACHER!" song. By comparison, species that nest in upper canopies of spruce forest, such as the bay-breasted warbler, employ weaker, higher-pitched songs.

If you don't recognize all the spring bird songs, that's okay. Just listen and enjoy them all. Once shrubs and trees are fully leafed, unobstructed views of birds are harder to obtain, but merely hearing a bird's song alerts us of its presence, which often results in direct sightings.

You can begin by listening to the abundant song sparrows around your neighborhood. The male songs have a structured pattern: a tripled introductory phrase, followed by warbles and a trailing trill at the end: "Maids, maids, maids, put on your tea-kettle, kettle, kettle." These sparrows have a dozen or more song variations. Males will switch song-endings after several repetitions, as competing males in surrounding territories follow each other's lead. This is called counter-singing. Give a listen this spring and, soon, you too will be birding by ear.

Celebrating the River

As a perpetual source of natural beauty, recreational opportunities, and commercial value, the Georges River comes alive each May as schools of alewives make their way upriver to spawn. Part of a 225-square-mile watershed, with origins at Lake Saint George in Liberty, the river takes a winding, forty-mile track through mixed forest habitats and fertile farmlands, emptying into Thomaston Harbor before widening its confluence into Muscongus Bay.

Since colonial times the alewife, a member of the herring family, has played a notable role in the town of Warren's traditional economy. Even the weathervane atop the town's fire station features an alewife motif. A dozen elver fishermen also place nets along the village shorelines to catch tiny, transparent "glass eels" that are shipped live to Asia.

In early mornings, squalling flocks of gulls and squadrons of double-crested cormorants filter upriver in anticipation of surging pulses of fish. Plunging-diving ospreys and cruising bald eagles create a stir, as they jockey for choice positions at the river's edge.

Amid the feathered morning chaos, some consistent behavior patterns emerge, and discernable pecking orders are established. The bald eagle is clearly the dominant player in all this. During an eagle approach, entire gull flocks take to simultaneous flight. And although eagles are fully capable of catching their own fish, they often pirate a meal from any fish-carrying osprey. Gaining altitude, the harassing eagles try to force ospreys to relinquish their catch. Eagles can retrieve a dropped fish in mid-air with remarkable agility and swiftness for such sizeable birds.

One afternoon I watched an immature eagle in hot pursuit of a protesting osprey. When the osprey resisted its thievery, the marauding eagle clutched onto the osprey's foot. The coupled raptors tumbled downward in cartwheel fashion for several hundred feet, still grappling when they plummeted out of sight.

Certain species seem to make best advantage of particular tidal cycles. Gulls seem most successful at low or mid-tides as they seize fish with their bill from the shallow water. With one gulp, the squirming fish is swallowed! In turn, opportunistic eagles can make a quick meal of an unwary gull or cormorant. Cormorants are probably safest from predation on the higher tides, when they can dive to elude an attack.

Living in Warren village, I enjoy daily opportunities to observe and study the river. Recently I gained other perspectives from an appreciative group of four wildlife photographers from Massachusetts, who had spent nearly a week around Warren photographing the springtime ospreys.

One photographer explained: "This is the third year I've come to Warren to photograph, and I look forward to this trip all winter. I have ospreys near my home, but I can get more close-up action shots here in a week than the entire year at home." Allowing for their lodging costs, meals, and other expenses for the week, the party spent an estimated thousand dollars in the midcoast. With its clean, healthy rivers and diverse wildlife resources, Maine generates $1.8 billion in eco-tourism dollars each year.

Chestnut on the Sides

If you happened to know this species' characteristic song, you could motor along most any secondary roadway in midcoast Maine in June and hear dozens of chestnut-sided warblers. Turn off your car radio and roll down the windows: "pleased, pleased, pleased to MEET-CHA!" resounds from shrubby wooded roadsides. The fortunes of this species have changed drastically since the clearing of mature evergreen forests in the early 1800's. As deciduous trees and second-growth habitats increased, the chestnut's numbers and range expanded north. Back then, the chestnut-sided was one of the rarest of wood warblers. Even John James Audubon saw only two or three of these warblers in his lifetime. Today the species nests from southern Canada throughout New England and down the spine of the Appalachians.

With so many small birds around in spring, a fixed definition of the term *wood-warbler* can be rather elusive. Strictly speaking, North American warblers are small-to-medium-sized birds with relatively thin bills designed for feeding on insects. These active, often brightly-colored birds have nine primary wing feathers; by contrast, most other songbirds have ten functional primaries. Ample research has been conducted on warblers, as progressively sophisticated DNA testing methods strive to decipher the lineal connections between the various species.

With extensive chestnut streaking along its neck and sides, the chestnut's breeding plumage illustrates its common given name. A yellow crown patch, black face stripe, and black-and-gold striped back complete the male's springtime look. By late summer, the species transitions to lime-green upper parts, a bold white eye-ring, and a light gray breast. These birds often create a distinct body profile by cocking their tails and drooping their wings.

Similar to various male warblers, the chestnut-sized performs a couple of differing songs between the spring and summer nesting seasons. The male's initial spring song is strongly accented to attract a breeding female into his territory. Later in the season, a less intense, alternate song is used to defend the territory from neighboring males.

The female takes about five days to build a loosely-woven, cupped nest of bark strips, weed stems, and finer grasses in shrubby habitat. Typically, the nests are placed one to three feet off the ground in roadside shrubs, briar tangles, and hedged undergrowth. Although well-hidden in dense cover, nests are often parasitized by brown-headed cowbirds. And, by the way, you won't need to crane your neck skyward to see these low-level warblers.

Connecting People with Birds

On occasion, *Free Press* readers play a role in determining the content of my bird articles. A recent example is a reader's inquiry about a roadside osprey nest in Bath: *In the lobby of Taste of Maine Restaurant there is a TV screen showing the osprey nest outside. Can you tell me what small bird has chosen to live underneath and inside the nest? There is a pair, and they remind me of a chickadee. They are in the lower left of the screen.*

Two Saturdays later, my wife and I stopped at the Taste of Maine on our way to Portland. I had some possible "suspects" in mind for this mystery identity quest, but remained uncertain about the eventual outcome. At the restaurant's parking lot, we watched an adult osprey in the nest above us as it stood to stretch and shift its incubating position. Soon enough, a sparrow-sized bird landed and perched just beneath the thick jumble of nest sticks. A male house sparrow, it passed through an opening at the base of the osprey nest, delivering a small feather to help cushion the interior of this temporary abode. Other deposits of weedy nesting materials would follow. Minutes later, its mate arrived, also gaining entrance to the inner sanctum of the bulky host nest.

Next we were joined by a tourist couple from Holland with obvious interest in observing the nesting raptors. Equipped with only a mobile phone, they seemed generally unfamiliar with ospreys in their native country. When my wife showed them an osprey image on her cell phone, the Dutch lady photographed the image for future reference. We then learned that this sojourning couple had made ten separate visits to the

U.S. Before departing, the gentleman returned from his rental car, carrying a fuzzy stuffed toy—a softball-sized bald eagle! He explained that this toy eagle had served as travel mascot on their previous visits to America.

Now let's focus on those squatting house sparrows, a.k.a. English sparrows. House sparrows were introduced into Brooklyn, New York, in 1851, with subsequent introductions in San Francisco and Salt Lake City in the 1870s. Currently, the species inhabits all parts of North America, except Alaska and far northern Canada. Extremely adaptable in their nest sites, they prefer human-made (or, in this case, osprey-made) structures such as eaves and walls of buildings, street lights, and an array of other creative nesting options. You may have heard and seen these noisy, chunky birds flitting through the interior rafters of big-box stores.

Why would these opportunistic sparrows select an osprey family as their landlords? Perhaps a better question is "Why not?" With the vigilant osprey pair presiding upstairs, the sparrows receive free security protection services from their capable raptor hosts. Upon arriving home, I check the bird literature: other osprey-sparrow nesting collaborations are well documented.

And, as a bonus, I charted dual nesting confirmations for the Maine Bird Atlas project. The ospreys and sparrows each earned "Occupied Nest" designations that confirm breeding activity. By the second year of the Atlas project, I'd confirmed ninety-three nesting species. I'm very pleased with my first "double-play" confirmations of this uniquely-shared nesting situation.

Eyes on the River

It's May again. In Warren village, the Georges River scene changes daily, as fresh-arriving galleries of birds exploit the annual alewife spawning runs. This spring transition is gradual at first, as legions of gangly double-crested cormorants make looping reconnaissance flights up river. Two weeks later, entire masses of birds will darken the dry surfaces of the river rocks.

Coming in squabbling daily flocks, herring gulls wheel overhead or paddle the alternate tide flows, clustering to rest and preen on village rooftops. Any fish captured by a gull is immediately swallowed whole or torn into bits, if other gulls join the fray.

Great blue herons, belted kingfishers, and swooping tree swallows cavort over the water. The swallows gather white, molted gull feathers to line their nesting cavities. Bald eagle numbers increase noticeably in May, mostly immature birds, still too young for nesting. A few other spring eagles may appear at the river, chocolate-toned fledglings from populations farther south. Florida eagles nest between October and March to avoid the torrid temperatures of summer. Maine's eaglets won't fledge until late July.

Eagles are agile fishers in their own right, but will frequently pirate fish from ospreys through extended, spiraling tail chases. Gulls and cormorants also become prey to eagles, when other suitable prey is lacking. Sunning snapping turtles and medium-sized swimming animals attempting a river crossing are fair game, as well.

Formerly called fish hawks, ospreys are significant players in the hectic spring equation. With their crook-winged silhouettes, ospreys exhibit a repertoire of conspicuous flight behaviors that make them intriguing to watch.

Male ospreys perform hovering sky dancing rituals several hundred feet above the river or nest site. With seesawing flight actions and dangled talons, the male often carries a fish aloft to tempt his mate. Hovering and soaring maneuvers are major components in the osprey's typical hunting strategies, as the birds scan from heights of thirty to one hundred feet. Once fully committed to a dive, the osprey folds back its wings and opens the talons of its trailing feet. Just before water impact, the osprey thrusts its long legs forward to grasp its prey beneath the water's surface. Although ospreys don't swim, they will float temporarily on the water with wings spread, before liftoff.

Barbed pads on the soles of the feet and a reversible outer toe allow the fish hawk to secure its slippery, squirming prey. For transport purposes, the fish is always aligned in a front-facing position to reduce wind resistance. Depending on the quantity of fish available, diving success varies between 25 and 70 percent. When alewives are schooling, single osprey dives can sometimes yield multiple catches of two or more fish.

Photographers enjoy the challenge of getting superior flight photos, shooting for that perfect image of the diving osprey with talons outstretched at the precise moment of contact between hawk and fish. Another highly-prized flight image is "the shake," a fleeting moment when the osprey—wait for it, wait for it—explosively shimmies its wet torso to shed the excess of dripping river water.

Gnatcatcher

Due to its minuscule size, this intriguing species may not be well known to some readers. And even for birders who are actively seeking it, this fidgety little bird can be quite challenging to locate in Maine. We are talking about a particular species of gnatcatcher.

The tiny blue-gray gnatcatcher is smaller than a chickadee, but has a feisty, lively demeanor worthy of a much larger bird. It is the most widespread member of its genus in North America, and the only one found in cold temperate regions. It is also the only truly migratory gnatcatcher, spending winters in the southern U.S. and Central America.

Some have described this gnatcatcher's appearance as resembling a miniature mockingbird in certain ways. Over a third of the bird's four-and-a-half-inch body length is taken up by its relatively long tail. The tail is frequently cocked at an angle and incessantly whipped from side to side and up and down. The flashed white outer tail feathers are assumed to help flush flying insects out of hiding.

Until recent decades, gnatcatchers were uncommon as far north as Maine. The Atlas of Breeding Birds in Maine project (1978–83), first confirmed gnatcatcher breeding in Maine in 1979. Prior to the 1950s, New Jersey was the northern extent of the breeding range, but limited nesting numbers now extend into southeastern Canada.

Male gnatcatchers are bluish above, darkest on the head and nape, and have white underparts. A black line extending from the bill to above and behind the eye creates a vaguely angry-looking expression. The bill is small and thin, a perfect feeding tool for grasping insects and spiders. Females are paler with a gray face, but both sexes feature a prominent white eye-ring.

Nesting in a variety of open deciduous woods settings, these gnatcatchers prefer moist areas with broad-leaved trees bordering habitat edges, such as power lines or parks. Gnatcatchers are occasional victims of brown-headed cowbirds that lay eggs in their nests. Can you picture the diminutive gnatcatcher parents scurrying around to provision a ravenous cowbird chick?

Although they are extremely vocal, the birds' high-pitched, wheezy song is at the higher end of the sound spectrum, but harsh-sounding scold notes are interspersed with its thin nasal call notes. Despite their vocalizing tendencies, however, gnatcatchers are quite easy to miss.

An exquisite compact nest of catkins, plant fibers, and bark is placed on high horizontal limbs, up to fifty feet above the ground. Built by both mates, the exterior nest is bound together with spider webbing and decorated with lichens. Gnatcatchers have the well-documented habit of tearing apart half-built or completed nests, and reusing the older materials in their subsequent nest. A camouflaged nest may appear as a small lump or gall on a branch. Probably the strongest chance of spotting a nest would be through careful observation of a parent bird carrying food to young. One year I was fortunate to find gnatcatcher pairs along Penbay Hospital's nature trails in Rockport and at Cramer Park near the Rockport village bridge.

Ravens' Grove

A decade ago, I began observing spring activities at a local raven nest. The birds' bulky dwelling was constructed of sizeable sticks, some an inch or more in diameter, collected directly from poplar, maple, and other nearby trees. If sticks drop to the ground during the building phase, ravens make no effort to retrieve them. Fresh or newly-added sticks are generally evident around the perimeters of active nests.

The ravens' two-foot-deep structure sat propped amid a cathedral stand of fifty-foot-tall white pines. Nests are typically lined with mud, strips of bark, grasses, deer hair, or collected bits of wool to help insulate the eggs. Once eggs are laid, they must be covered and protected from the cold overnight conditions of early spring. In previous years, the incubating parent usually faced in a westerly direction in the nest. This time, she was oriented eastward. Traditional nest sites, some built on steep cliffs, are commonly occupied through successive generations, with a preferable mile of distance between sites.

The common raven is the largest member of the corvid family. Its eastern members include the familiar American crow, fish crow, blue jay, and Canada (or gray) jay. Adult ravens are hardy creatures that remain paired throughout their lifetimes. In February, pairs begin early preparation for the nesting session. Courtship behaviors, such as close, mutual soaring activities and vocalizations, serve as pair-bonding rituals. Other bonding behaviors include allopreening, in which partners delicately preen the head and body feathering of its mate. The male may also feed the female as she mimics the begging behavior of young, dependent birds. Being agile, powerful flyers, pairs engage in choreographed aerial tumbles, barrel rolls, and playful, abrupt plummets on windy days.

Ravens are distinguished from crows by their larger size, massive head, and heavier bill. In flight, the large head, longer, pointed wings, and wedge-shaped tail are useful clues to identification. Males are noticeably larger, with deeper, croaking voices, than females.

By mid-March, this local pair often perched near their intended nest site and, soon thereafter, the top of the incubating female's head became visible above the nest rim. Throughout the incubation period, the male provides her with food. Clutch sizes vary from three to five greenish, mottled eggs that are incubated by the female for eighteen to nineteen days. The omnivorous ravens actively hunt for small rodents or scavenge within their territories for carrion, fruits, or berries. They will pirate food items from other birds as well.

On May 1, I entered the ravens' grove in the early morning. With only her head and neck exposed, the female sat quietly inside the shadow-darkened nest, paying me little mind. At times she preened, shifted her weight, or poked her stout bill into the nest lining. A chunk of red meat rested on one edge of the nest. Standing up, she began tearing off tiny bits of the flesh, feeding her chicks with jabbing head movements. I glimpsed the two chicks' bare pinkish heads as they gaped toward the parent's mouth. Maybe two weeks-old, the chicks squabbled in earnest competition for the meat scraps.

The wide-foraging male raven now returned, making booming croaks and "kronk" sounds that penetrated and echoed through the entire grove. Sensing a human presence, he was sending a threatening message of unwelcome. Two crows arrived to harass him with their shrill, cawing calls and erratic flight attacks. Unperturbed, the huge raven deposited another piece of meat on the lip of the nest. Then, circling tightly above the nest tree, the raven issued several more piercing yells. Taking his obvious hint to heart, I left the busy pair to their parental chores.

Roadkills

Driving a section of Route17 one early-May morning, I encountered an all-too-familiar sight: a brownish mat of windblown feathers that lay on the median strip. And, better or worse, my curiosity reigns supreme whenever I approach a lifeless figure on a roadway. Traveling at road speed, I couldn't fathom this oddly-shaped configuration of feathers. What was it? Uncertain, I circled back to check.

With its cat-like ear tufts in conspicuous view, it was a great horned owl that had been struck by a passing vehicle. It's not uncommon to find owls, especially roadside hunters like barred owls, as traffic victims. But this particular incident was strangely different, since it involved two separate species in the same fatal crash. The dead owl lay united with its dawn victim, an American crow, clenched permanently in its locked talons. Seeing the hapless pair entwined on the pavement, one could only imagine the instantaneous thudding shock experienced by the pre-dawn driver.

Following the development of the internal combustion engine and automobile, the naturalist Joseph Grinnell noted in 1920: "This [roadkill] is a relatively new source of fatality; and if one were to estimate the entire mileage of such roads in the state [of California], the mortality must mount into the hundreds and perhaps thousands every 24 hours."

And the rest is history, as they say. Acknowledging other well-documented causes of bird deaths tied to humans, only cats and collisions with buildings produce more deaths than traffic incidents. Our modern highway system is essential to human need, but certain design-safety features of today's roads may inadvertently contribute to bird mortality. Highway rumble strips installed to provide a tactile, vibrating alert to lane-drifting drivers could play some role. Winter gravel and road salt deposits accumulate in the road grooves, attracting both small and large wildlife in search of grit and salt intake, while exposing wildlife to road dangers.

Perhaps one positive aspect of roadkills is the carrion it produces for scavengers such as vultures, crows, ravens, and carnivorous mammals such as foxes. Hence, we see increasing numbers of turkey vultures and occasional black vultures in the state. Have you noticed pairs of common ravens that routinely patrol certain sections of highway? They are scanning for pickup meals within their territories. Gray squirrel, anyone?

But can birds and animals somehow "learn to avoid" the inherent dangers of highways? Birds do appear to adapt to some emergent challenges. How about that adventuresome American robin or phoebe nesting in close proximity to your porch? But busy highways present unique challenges of their own, as birds focus on pursuing aerial insects or mammal prey across lanes of traffic.

Ecologist Charles Brown studied road fatalities of cliff swallows in Nebraska. These swift-flying swallows often nest on buildings close to highways, where they swoop low to catch insects. "When the researchers looked back at the numbers of swallows collected as roadkill each year, they found that the count had steadily declined from twenty fatalities a season in 1984 and 1985 to less than five per season for each of the next five years. During that same time, the number of nests and birds had more than doubled, and the amount of traffic in the area had remained steady." This study continued for thirty years.

Deeper analysis revealed the birds that were being killed weren't representative of the rest of the population. On average, the killed birds had longer wings, making them less agile and fractionally slower to swerve away from oncoming cars. Had the surviving swallows' wings evolved structurally, reducing wing-size over those intervening thirty years, or had they just learned better survival tactics to avoid getting struck?

Ruff Around the Edges

Birding is a fascinating pastime for a good number of reasons. Since it connects birds, people, and the given circumstances of the moment, any day afield can bring unexpected adventures and some surprising outcomes.

The early morning of May 19, 2017, is a case in point. During a brief morning stop at the Weskeag Marsh parking area on my drive to work, I met a birder from Connecticut who had noticed a shorebird gathering in the front pools. He was wondering about one of the birds. When I scoped the pool, a medium-sized dark-backed shorebird drew my instant attention. This bird's unique field characteristics, the chestnut-colored neck and black splotching on the white belly, made for a relatively straightforward identification. Its pot-bellied look, and orangey bill and legs were the clinchers. It was a ruff!

Rare but somewhat regular in Maine, ruffs are an Old World species that typically winters in Europe and Asia before migrating to spring breeding grounds in the Arctic. Only seven sightings had been recorded in the state since 2000, mostly from Scarborough, Weskeag, and the Penjajawoc Marshes. My longtime birding friend Mark Libby and I had recorded a Weskeag ruff fifteen to twenty years earlier, a young male that had landed practically at our feet. There are an estimated 30 + state records, with approximately seven records since 2000 (Sheehan/Bevier), most found in Weskeag, Scarborough, and Penjajawoc Marshes, important refuges for shorebirds.

The ruff's elaborate breeding plumages are accentuated by streaming head plumes and a thick collar of fluffy neck feathers that give the bird its common name. Ruffs come in a variety of body colors, trending between black, white, and rufous shades. On the breeding grounds, groups of ruffs assemble in collective courtship circles called *leks* to compete for the females, known as reeves.

I phoned Louis Bevier, a member of the Maine Bird Records Committee, who referred the sighting to the Maine Birds hotline. Hotline rarities often elicit large turnouts of birders from across the region. In certain instances, as with a rare nesting species, it is often best not to reveal sensitive nest locations that could endanger the welfare or breeding success of the bird. Since the ruff was on definite transit through our area, the sighting was worth sharing with all.

Hoping to get some documentation photos of this rare shorebird, I hit my camera's switch button. What's this? Despite my usual regular battery recharging routines, the camera's battery was dead! And I had no spare battery onsite.

Meanwhile, I quickly returned home to grab a portable battery charger cord. By the time I'd reached Weskeag again, the battery had charged well enough to take a few photos.

Then another issue emerged. How close should one approach a feeding ruff to obtain decent documentation photos, without potentially frightening him away? Moving too close could flush the bird, depriving others of seeing him. I knew this would be a life bird for many birders who would come looking for it.

For much of the time, the ruff kept its head low, picking through the muddy grasses in company with two species of yellowlegs. This vantage gave extended opportunities for species size and behavior comparisons. Advancing cautiously, I paused as the bird entered the back of a roadside pool, where it stood and preened in a background of reflected water. That was close enough.

As for the birders? Oh, yes, they came by the dozens during the two days the bird remained. I spoke with one birder from Jay, Maine, who'd driven an hour and a half to see the ruff. He spent a half hour savoring the life-bird moment and then announced, "Well, I've got to get back to work now." "So should I," I said.

Safe and Sound

As the May season progresses, serious threats can result from predacious species, intent on devouring eggs or young. A variety of hungry mammals, such as foxes and raccoons, busily patrol the scene as well. Red squirrels reportedly consume a high percentage of all woodland birds' eggs.

But what about our unintended human contacts with nesting birds? Last week, I stumbled upon a killdeer's nest at a vacant children's playground. The nest was concealed in thick layers of wood chips covering the ground. I heard shrill, protesting vocalizations, before eventually spotting the fast-closing plover pair. Judging from their animated distress level, I must have been in the vicinity of the camouflaged nest itself (which I didn't attempt to locate.) One of the rushing adults began a distraction display quite near my feet. During distraction displays, killdeer and other members of the plover family hobble and adopt tilting, lop-sided body postures, feigning a broken wing. Its trailing right wing was draped in a pathetic manner, and the back feathers were puffed high. Its rich, reddish tail was fanned in dramatic fashion to deflect my attention from the nest area.

Killdeer lay four large eggs in a shallow scrape of bare ground, with little or no nest lining. The twenty-four to twenty-six-day incubation process is delayed until the clutch is completed, so that the four downy chicks will hatch simultaneously. As such, the precocial hatchlings are superbly mobile from the start, able to forage independently or scamper into protective cover when necessary.

Other species use similar measures to protect their young. While jogging, I once encountered a family of ruffed grouse, as a hen grouse led her dozen fuzzy chicks across a dirt roadway. Heeding the parent's squeaky, high-pitched alarms, each chick vanished before my eyes, hiding beneath blankets of fallen oak leaves.

The grouse chicks were safe then, but my troubles were only beginning. The mother grouse mounted a physical aerial attack. Vocalizing forcefully, the grouse flew repeatedly at my face, brushing me with her wings. My only defense was in shielding my face from the blows and leaning forward as I sprinted away. Following her fifty-yard pursuit, the agitated grouse relented.

But if you're seeking a genuinely threatening experience, the northern goshawk can deliver it. Goshawks are the largest member of the Accipiter clan. Built with relatively short wings and a long tail for steering through dense cover, goshawks inhabit secluded stands of mature conifer and hardwood forest. They capture prey in short bursts of blurring speed, often scooting between branches and crashing through thickets. Their principle diet consists of grouse, crows, snowshoe hares, squirrels, and other small rodents.

Years ago I discovered a goshawk nest (I should more correctly state that the hawks discovered me.) When I inadvertently approached the nest site, the hawk pair issued rapid-fire "cak-cak-cak" threat calls—warning shots across my bow. Their nest of small sticks was located in a tall yellow birch just inside the trail, thirty yards ahead. By now, both glaring adults had advanced and were perched directly above my head. The female member was especially intimidating as she extended her right foot downward in my direction. For added emphasis, she squeezed her hooked talons open and shut several times. Females are, on average about 25 percent larger than males. They are generally more aggressive in guarding the nest, and are more likely to make physical contact with careless intruders. Not turning my back on the pair for one instant, I cautiously backed away. Message received.

Sherm's Worms

My friend Sherm Hoyt had mentioned the congregations of gulls converging on mudflats below his home on Upper Long Cove in St. George. He explained that sandworms were spawning there as they do each spring, and that hundreds of gulls were exploiting these ephemeral, wriggling bonanzas. The best time to witness this chaotic scene was about an hour before low tide, he said.

The sandworm, *Neresis virens*, is a marine organism that lives in burrows of sand or mud. Length and color vary greatly, but the general color is a metallic green. Male worms swarm around egg-laying females and deposit lines of sperm along the mudded bottom. After completing their fertilization duties, the dilapidating males' bodies turn a darker shade, and they die.

Sandworms provide significant ecological benefit for other invertebrates, fish, gulls, and shorebirds. Their commercial value as fishing bait is also a cog in Maine's coastal economy. Spawning activity is likely related to several factors. Optimal water temperature for spawning is generally around seven to eight degrees centigrade. Spawning activity also aligns with phases of full-moon and new-moon cycles, occurring during the higher water "spring tides."

The afternoon of April 8, 2016 was warm and sunny when I arrived at the St. George site with my camera in tow. About a foot of remaining water covered the mudflats as a few eager gulls plunged downward to snatch the six-to-ten-inch-long worms from beneath the surface.

Noticing that most of the gull flocks were assembled on the opposite shoreline, I decided that my 400 mm camera lens was of limited use, and quickly abandoned delusions of capturing *National Geographic* quality photos. Perhaps the bigger story lay in the waters directly before me.

I eased down toward the water's edge. Whoa! Scores of sandworms were swimming and spawning, literally at my feet! Some worms swam in straight lines, while others swam in tight, hula-like orbits. Each individual was occupied with its purposeful work, that of reproduction.

A large female sandworm wagged her fringed body in an egg-laying cadence near an edge of seaweed. I witnessed her tiny eggs dropping like silent little bombshells onto the sediment of bottom. Male worms circulated everywhere, issuing whitish sperm from their posterior ends. The fertilization process appeared somewhat random, like squadrons of slow-motion planes, skywriting in white dots and dashes against the dark, mudded background.

With low-drain tide approaching, the remaining waters evacuated rapidly down the cove's shallow, sloped basin. The pace and movement of the worms slowed, while taking on a greater urgency and poignancy, as well. Male worms struggled vainly against the inevitable fatigue of dying, as their strained swimming motions gradually lost effectiveness. Soon legions of corpses lay exposed on the open mud.

But now, I was puzzled. Despite the glut of food available, very few gulls came to dine at the banquet. Why not, I wondered? Had several days of gorging on worms quelled the appetites of the ravenous birds? From experience with gulls, that idea seemed unlikely. Perhaps a future day of observation would provide a better answer.

Wet Weather Birding

For several springs, I led five-day Spring Birding in Maine programs for the Elderhostel (now Road Scholars program). Based in Camden, we surveyed birding hotspots throughout the midcoast in search of anything wearing feathers. The program especially appealed to West Coast birders seeking the wide variety of spring warblers found in the Northeast (up to twenty-five-plus warbler species are possible in mid-May). And, of course, the obligatory Atlantic puffins were high on most wish lists.

Living on the Atlantic coastline, Mainers come to anticipate the changeable weather conditions of spring days. This concept was put to the test one May, when heavy, windswept rainfall persisted for the entire week. So what did our groups do all that week? We worked a bit harder and smarter to keep ourselves and our equipment relatively dry. And, yes, we went outside and found birds! Our forays on foot were brief, but were tightly focused on specific habitat types. Since most birds favor particular types of habitat, it often pays dividends to visit multiple habitats. Taking advantage of the rain-saturated ground conditions at a Rockland athletic field, we discovered an uncommon lesser black-backed gull feasting on flooded-out earthworms.

Most bird activity is driven by their essential need to find food, particularly during harsh weather conditions that can rapidly deplete energy reserves. Our birding group sought out places along sheltered, wooded trails that were generally out of the direct line of brisk winds. We listened intently for bird song, and followed up on the slightest of vocalizations.

In a group setting, there is always the added benefit of having more eyes and ears to scan the scene.

Our original schedule had called for a day trip to Monhegan Island to visit one of the Northeast's premier birding hotspots. With steady rain, southeast winds at thirty-five miles per hour and fifteen-foot seas, however, going to the island was totally out of the question. So we boarded two vans and headed down to Evergreen Cemetery, a majestic 239-acre green space located off Stevens Avenue in Portland. Maine's largest cemetery features four ponds, rows of stately trees, and a network of wooded trails that are often teeming with spring migrants.

Hunkering beneath some of those huge trees, our group slowly made its way around the perimeter of the largest pond at the rear of the cemetery. Nearby, a spotted sandpiper bobbed and teetered on a floating log. Rufous-sided towhees chanted their repetitive "drink-your-teeee" songs from dense cover. We soon connected with groups of foraging warblers that fed low in the shrubby forest cover, many at eye-level.

In windy or wet weather conditions, insects stay closer to the ground to escape the upper elements. At such times, the birds logically follow suit. As the rains intensified, we returned to the vans to eat our boxed lunches. From the warm interiors of the vans, we watched as over a dozen species of colorful, breeding-plumaged warblers darted for insects on the grassy lawns just a few feet away. Participants from western regions were dumbstruck by this living spectacle. One California birder enthused, "These eastern warblers REALLY DO exist! These are the best views of warblers I have ever had!"

Woodcock!

Driving to Bangor in March, I spotted an American woodcock feeding close to the margins of busy Route 1 in Searsport. With little time to spare and scant space to pull safely off the highway, I kept motoring. On my return trip three hours later, however, the bird hadn't budged, as it nuzzled for worms in a small muddy seep of snow melt a few feet off the pavement.

Try as I might, I could think of no compelling reason (aside from the thrum of heavy traffic and a limited pull-off zone) why I shouldn't just hit the brake and position my vehicle for some easy photos of the probing "timberdoodle". After all, woodcocks are generally reclusive creatures that offer few unobstructed views or extended opportunities for clinical behavior-watching.

Let's consider this intriguing species from stem to stern. Woodcocks are plump, short-necked members of the shorebird family that live in upland terrains. Unlike the typically long-winged structure of many shorebirds, woodcocks have short, rounded wings that function efficiently in tightly wooded settings. The outer wing has three narrow primary feathers that produce a twittering sound during the bird's dawn and dusk ascents. The stubby woodcock tail is fanned out during the ground-based phases of its courtship.

Except for the nasal "peent" calls and occasional chuckled notes given by courting males, the species' song repertoire is rudimentary. However, its crepuscular vocal and aerial courtship displays are well worth your attention in spring.

The woodcock's "upside-down" brain configuration is truly unique among birds. As an adaptation to its feeding style, the cerebellum, which manages muscle coordination and balance, is located just above the spinal column rather than at the rear of the skull. The woodcock's large eyes are set high and far back on the head, providing a 360-degree horizontal plane for monitoring danger while probing in damp substrates. The over-sized eyes are very useful tools during the low-light periods, when woodcocks are most active.

The tip of the woodcock's long, flexible bill functions like a set of tweezers. Additionally, its prehensile bill is packed with sensory receptors for detecting and grabbing earthworms beneath the soil surface.

I watched closely as the roadside bird inserted its bill deep in the muddy ground, apparently unfazed by nearby rumbling highway trucks and whizzing cars. Five inches of fresh snow had fallen, but these hardy shorebirds make mid-March arrivals in Maine. This woodcock's foraging success became evident as the bird extracted one earthworm after another from the wet decaying leaf litter.

If you've not witnessed the woodcock's odd, syncopated walking gait, you must! This is a deliberate, body-rocking motion as the bird steps heavily with its alternate foot. Theory has it that these rhythmic motions cause earthworms to move around in the soil and reveal their presence. Species of plovers perform similar foot-tapping maneuvers that trigger prey exposures.

Ending its several-hour feeding session, the woodcock's body began to bob again, as it slothfully exited the mudded depression. Where was it headed now? The bird padded up a slight incline, its feet sporadically breaking through the loose snow cover. I pondered its halting exertions. Would a short burst of flight have been more efficient, and perhaps conserved some physical energy? The woodcock continued to tread the fluffy snow depths, eventually reaching cover beneath a spruce bow farther up the hill. Undoubtedly, this resourceful bird had a survival strategy beyond my feeble human reckoning. Securing its encampment near a reliable hotbed of worm activity, where it could resume the wriggling feast the next morning, made perfect sense.

PART II

Summer Sightings

A Nesting Report Card

As July began, the 2019 Maine nesting season reached an approximate halfway point in some respects. Certain of the earliest nesters, such as American robins, had already fledged their first clutches, and were gearing up for a second go. Other species were at various stages in nesting progress.

For the second year, I was involved with the Maine Bird Atlas project, a five-year volunteer study to assess the abundance and distribution of nesting species across the state. The project's descriptive breeding codes set the criteria for evaluating breeding success. Evidence of breeding falls into three categories: Possible, Probable, or Confirmed Breeding. Several species of woodpeckers nest around my Warren neighborhood, including downy, hairy, yellow-bellied sapsucker, and red-bellied. The red-bellied pair occupies a cavity in a tall willow tree near my house. Earlier in the season, I'd witnessed the pair sharing time together. These observations earned them a Possible Breeding category: "In Appropriate Habitat." Once they settled into the nest hole, I upgraded their status to Probable Breeding: "Visiting Probable Nest Site." Then in late June, the pair rated a Confirmed Breeding status under two separate code designations: "Carrying Food" (to young) and then "Recently Fledged Young."

The specific timeframes of nesting activity are tied to individual species. Within each species, however, we see some slight variations in timing and nesting progress. In late June of 2019, I discovered two different pairs of nesting cedar waxwings in separate phases of the nesting cycle.

One pair was already feeding its young (FY code), while the second pair was still building a nest (NB). The details of this particular building project were fascinating to watch. Apparently for convenience sake, the waxwings had stockpiled a fist-sized cluster of tinsel-length plastic strands next to their partially constructed nest. The busy pair consolidated natural grasses and plant fibers into the bourgeoning nest, with alternate placements of plastic strands woven masterfully into place.

Later that day, I discovered a sora in a flooded, abandoned gravel pit. Nicknamed "marsh chicken," soras are small, secretive rails that inhabit shallow, fresh-water wetlands with emergent vegetation. The bird's stubby yellow bill and black facial mask are standout features of an otherwise brownish body within stands of cattails. Hearing descending whinnies and high pitched "ker-wheer" call notes, I located an adult sora feeding amid the thick cover. Then, to my delight, a black downy sora chick flushed from the same patch of vegetation. The fledgling chick fluttered along weakly for fifty feet before plummeting into protective vegetation. In this case, the confirmed breeding code was an easy one: "Recently Fledged Young."

A belted kingfisher pair had excavated a nest burrow in the steep upper banking of the pit. Color-wise, kingfishers could be mistaken for a quirky blue jay with an over-sized shaggy head crest and heavier bill. The male kingfisher's white underparts are bisected by a single bluish belly band. In a plumage role-reversal of sorts, the female kingfisher has an additional broad, rusty belly band, making her more colorful than her mate.

Broadcasting their chattering, rattled calls, both kingfishers returned at intervals to deliver small fish into the nest burrow. As you would have guessed, the kingfishers' actions around the nest confirmed their breeding status: CF for carrying food.

Antics

One summer, a family of American crows nested behind my house. After hearing the nestlings' persistent begging calls for several weeks, I saw they had assembled themselves throughout the neighborhood.

I observed an interesting bit of corvid behavior as the troupe of six crows landed on my front lawn, launching into vigorous pursuit of insects. Their animated activity seemed direct and purposeful. An adult crow appeared to be shuffling some form of insect prey toward the submissive, quivering youngsters. But feeding of young was not the prime motive behind this active scene. A week earlier, I'd patched a hole in the lawn with sandy gravel, and a small ant colony had established itself within the circle of freshly-packed dirt.

One crow belly-flopped onto the dirt patch, fanning out its wings and tail to a wide-angled position. Now I recognized what was happening here: the crow was anting! For several minutes, the bird remained immobile, adopting a trance-like state, bill slightly ajar and torso arched in a rigid, upright posture. Then a second crow assumed a similar position, pressing its body firmly against the ground, and simultaneously burying its face in the lawn grass.

What is anting? Anting is a self-help behavior, in which birds utilize ants to rid themselves of lice and feather mites, or possibly ease resulting skin irritations during feather molt. Since nests are notorious havens for mites and other skin parasites, newly-fledged birds can be afflicted with itchy skin. Uncontrolled numbers of mites can reportedly destroy wing feathers.

Biologists recognize two modes of anting behavior: active and passive. In theory, here's how it works: During active anting sessions, birds pick up ants with their bills, sometimes crushing the ants and rubbing the acidic chemical secretions into wing and body feathers. Live ants are also applied directly to itchy areas. When certain species of ants are disturbed or injured, they emit formic acid, a naturally occurring insecticide and fungicide. The concentration of formic acid emitted by ants exceeds 50 percent, which has been shown to be powerful enough to kill fleas and mites.

The passive anting approach is markedly different. Birds simply settle onto an anthill while flaring out their wings and tail, encouraging ants to swarm throughout their feathers. Often the anting bird will squirm, flop, or thrash about, to instigate ant reactions. Most anting sessions last for three to five minutes. Once engaged in anting sessions, birds may persist in the activity, even in the face of potential danger or human approach.

In earlier June, I had observed a third anting episode, where a crow had mounted a massive four-foot hill of Allegheny mound ants at a wood's edge. The Allegheny ant is a largely beneficial species that consumes arthropods on Maine's wild blueberry barrens. The crow's exaggerated behavior drew my eye as it rolled onto its side, vigorously slapping its wings against the dome of the hill. After several minutes of focused anting activity, the crow retreated to a spruce to preen.

More than two hundred avian species, mostly songbirds, have been documented in anting. In the absence of ants, birds may substitute centipedes, moth balls, citrus fruits, vinegar, and still-glowing fire embers to get relief. Be on the lookout for this unique and fascinating behavior at an anthill near you.

Banded Birds

When scanning flocks of birds, I follow a long-held practice: I focus strict attention on their feet and legs. Surely each species has a unique set of legs, functionally adapted to its lifestyle, but that's not really my matter of interest. I'm searching for leg bands placed there by banders and researchers. These colored leg bands bear distinguishing numerical and alphabetic codes. Brightly-toned, little flags on shorebird legs are generally the easier to spot and decipher. Southbound shorebirds are netted in gossamer-like mist nets strung along coastal beachfronts. Captured birds are carefully removed from the nets, measured and aged, and banded. Using my 30x spotting scope, I try to read band inscriptions. And a documenting photograph of the bird in question is always a plus. All reports of banded birds can be forwarded to a web database called Bandedbirds.org.

One mid-July encounter at Weskeag Marsh several years ago involved a migrant short-billed dowitcher. Foraging with a group of six other dowitchers, its lime green leg flag lettering was readily apparent through my spotting scope: "AUC." The banding history of this migrant bird was as follows: originally captured and flagged at North Beach Island in Chatham, Massachussets, on July 31, 2016, the dowitcher was sighted again at Chatham on August 3, 2016. Its Weskeag occurrence was just the second sight recovery record for this particular individual.

Other banded sightings? Since 2012, I've observed a leg-banded ring-billed gull that spends the late summers through early spring in a tight little territory around the Rockland McDonald's. By now, gull BF2Z is an old acquaintance of mine. He's an adult male gull that journeys annually to an island nesting colony outside Montreal, Canada, that hosts forty-five thousand gull pairs. In May 2018, BF2Z was recorded at the Canada colony. Then on July 7, I spied his blue leg band as he perched atop his favorite utility pole at his favorite parking lot in Rockland. I send occasional updated sighting reports to the Canadian biologist who captains this international gull study. In turn, he provides me with sightings dates from the Montreal island site. Migration studies reveal strong "site fidelity" among various species of gulls, documenting a tendency to return consistently to specific locations.

Since most metallic leg-band numbers are too minute for visual detection, the majority of band recoveries are inadvertent, the result of finding the corpse of a deceased bird. Back in 1991, my birding friend Mark Libby and I found a dead, banded royal tern at Popham Beach following a powerful August ocean storm. The tern had apparently blown northward, and had succumbed to the punishing conditions. Mark forwarded the band recovery information to the U.S. Fish & Wildlife Banding Lab in Laurel, Maryland.

The surprising back story of this young tern was compelling, and of special personal interest to each of us. According to the Banding Lab certificate, a gentleman named John Weske had banded this juvenile tern at Lola, North Carolina, two months earlier. A note on the recovery certificate read: "It was too young to fly when banded." We both knew that, for some years, John Weske had banded hundreds of juvenile terns at this southern beach location. How did Mark and I know such information? John was a mutual friend, who summered at his family cottage in nearby Chamberlain, Maine.

Chasing Loons

In mid-July of 2012, I accompanied Mark DiGirolamo during his annual loon monitoring studies for the Biodiversity Research Institute (BRI), which is funded by the U.S. Fish & Wildlife Service. This work involves surveys of adult and juvenile common loon populations on eleven ponds in Waldo County, Maine. Our first stop was Sanborn Pond, north of Brooks. Two adult loons dived at the back of this eighty-seven-acre pond, where two fuzzy chicks paddled lazily and sunned themselves a few yards away.

In many ways, this tranquil scene represents a triumph of nature's powerful recovery mechanisms. In September 2001, an oil tanker truck drove off highway 137, rolling into the pond and spilling approximately fifty-five-hundred gallons of toxic fuel oil into the waters. In the following two years, nesting mortalities temporarily halted loon breeding activity there.

Next we traveled to Unity Pond, where Mark launched his small motorized boat. We soon sighted two parent loons, accompanying a single chick in a side cove. The adult female loon was already familiar to Mark. Displaying a bright yellow leg band, she had been banded at her nest earlier in the season. Capturing and banding of loons is usually accomplished at night, as birds sit tightly on the nest. Capturing a diving loon on open water is entirely a different matter.

We drifted closer to the threesome, only to discover that the male adult was also banded: a blue-over-green band arrangement of dual leg bands. This was a bird of unknown origins that could be identified later by checking historical banding records. The loon chick hung close to the male bird, before relaxing and tucking its head to nap. Adult male loons can weigh up to twelve pounds.

Nests are located at or near the water's edge, with incubating birds facing the water for rapid escape. Loons' over-sized webbed feet are positioned far back on their body, and walking on land is cumbersome. Wooded islands, shielded from wind and wave action, are often favored nest locations. The nest structure itself may begin as simple bare ground, with vegetation added throughout the average twenty-nine-day incubation process. Man-made loon nesting rafts also attract a few nesting pairs.

We headed up pond, looking at distant birds sitting on the pond's glassy surface. Two pairs of adults and a fifth lone individual occupied the middle portion of the pond. Mark had tediously calculated the territorial boundaries between the pairs, and he felt there was potentially enough space to support an additional breeding pair. Again, we checked for leg bands on each diving loon. In their manner of diving, loons compress the body feathers, lean forward, and basically "sink" below the surface, giving only limited opportunities to spot a leg band. In terms of providing logistical and biological data, however, each banded bird is worth its weight in gold.

With flooding rains and high water levels in June 2012, the early loon nesting season proved to be challenging for them. Some pairs abandoned their nests entirely. In such dire circumstances, the question is always the same: Would the loons attempt to re-nest within the same season? Mark had already collected two loon eggs (a federal permit is required to collect any eggs) from an abandoned nest site at Cross Pond in Morrill. These eggs had been submersed in water and were no longer viable.

Facing threats from predators, nest disturbances, fluctuating water levels, and environmental contaminants, common loons are still the icons of Maine wilderness. Get out there and savor their eerie, evening yodels from a summer lakeside.

From Russia with Love

Over several decades of birding activity, some interesting field opportunities have come my way. Back in 1992, National Audubon Society's Senior Vice President of Education Marshall Case invited me to lead a field trip for two Russian ornithologists and three teenaged Russians birders. A video cameraman and the host of a popular Russian television nature program were also part of the visiting entourage.

This period in history had ushered in a new spirit of openness between Russian and U.S. societies, and Mr. Case had made several trips to Russia to tour some nature centers, where promising young ornithologists were studying. He determined that, despite their lack of the high-tech birding optics and the modern field guides available to most American birders, the Russian kids had developed remarkable field identification skills through live field experiences and direct observations.

The Russian group was lodged at National Audubon's Hog Island Camp in Bremen. Since it was late August, we visited Weskeag Marsh to witness the height of the summer shorebird migration. The two Russian ornithologists had very contrasting personalities. The older man's demeanor was decidedly reserved, and apparently he spoke limited English. His younger counterpart had an outgoing personality and a friendly, talkative manner. His eyes widened as he pointed enthusiastically toward a small yellow-and-black bird in undulating flight: "American goldfinch!" he shouted. It was a "life bird" for this excited member of the Russian National Academy of Sciences. Back home in

Russia, the red-faced European goldfinch would be a more typical sighting. Later, I asked this younger scientist if he might eventually return to America in the future. "No," he replied with some hesitation, "The rest of my life is already scheduled."

Of necessity, the Russian group was traveling light, and Audubon had purchased pairs of inexpensive "throw-away" sneakers for each birder to wear in the smelly salt marsh mud. As we prepared to enter the marsh, however, I gained deeper perspective into the Russians' true situation. Everyone, including the two eminent ornithologists, quickly removed their shoes and rolled up their pant legs to wade barefooted into the gooey mud. Each of the valued pair of new sneakers remained neatly stowed in the cardboard shoe boxes inside the van.

Out in the marsh, we soon encountered a dozen migrant shorebird species amid groups of white egrets and grayish herons. One of the teens crept stealthily toward a roosted greater yellowlegs and took a photo with his disposable camera. Having studied them in similar habitats in Russia, these precocious teens were already familiar with both species of yellowlegs and several of the plovers and sandpipers we discovered at the high-tide roost sites.

Completing our field session, the television host asked me to describe some of the birds we had just seen for the video camera. She explained that our field trip experience would be edited and broadcast to an approximate audience of ten million Russian viewers. As I tried my best to make impromptu comments about our experience, the host graciously reassured me: "Don't worry. It will all be dubbed into Russian." That seemed only fitting, since bird-speak should always be an international language.

Good for the Heart

In my personal life there have been few times when I've felt disconnected from birds, wildlife, and natural habitats. These things satisfy my intuitive need for natural connections and experiences.

How might you feel if your access to birds and wildlife was cut off by some odd sets of circumstances? What if a sizeable number of animal species went extinct within your lifetime, or your children's lifetimes? Would that matter to you in any significant way? Would that create a discernable void in the quality of your daily life?

My accustomed string of bird sightings was suspended on June 3, 2016, as I was wheeled into a cardiothoracic surgical suite at Maine Medical Center for an aortic valve replacement. No outside window views from there. Instead, only clusters of piercingly brilliant surgical lights and a team of green-clad medical professionals waiting at their appointed stations.

Following my successful surgery, open-sky views from my patient rehabilitation room left much to be desired: just a square window across the room with an exterior alcove leading toward angular metal rooflines and flat, pebbled roof terrains. Hemmed in by six to eight stories of vertical walls, I was prepared to spend some extended time there without birds, without nature.

Then an animated voice issued from the outer hallway: "Look at the two baby pigeons outside on the roof! The parents are feeding them!"

"Oh, yes, I can see them!" added a second excited viewer. "Over in that shady corner. They have pin-feathers and can't be more than a couple of days old."

An unanticipated birding opportunity had presented itself in this otherwise cloistered, sterile setting. Hauling myself out of bed, I padded into the outer hallway for a peek. Yes, the pebbled roof habitat was certainly conducive for pigeons: "Nests on window ledges, crevices in buildings, under bridges, in barns." "Nest is shallow, flimsy platform of carelessly arranged grasses, straws, debris."

Originally introduced from Europe several hundred years ago, rock pigeons have existed in the city of Portland for dozens of decades. While they're dismissed as potential disease spreaders and general pests by some people, I wasn't in a position to quibble at this particular juncture. Beyond my early recovery milestones, like bathing myself, shaving, or walking without assistance for the first time, this was a definite normalizing experience for me, emotionally therapeutic and nourishing in the fullest sense.

Checking online later, I learned of a "Pigeons of Portland Maine Facebook" page, where folks could post their pigeon photos. And why not? Everyone else seems to use Facebook these days, posting highlighted selfies and video accounts.

In the next moment, a passing hospital administrator entered the hallway area, apparently leading a facility tour for a visiting medical dignitary. Noting the growing hubbub around the pigeon viewers, she nodded to the guest, saying, "We are very proud of our pigeons."

After I returned home, I saw scores of birds in my neighborhood. The future looks bright for many species, and cautiously guarded for others. Science-based watch lists developed by the National Audubon Society and the American Bird Conservancy reveal the stiff survival challenges facing a number of these species. But think about it another way: If you arrived at Baskins Robbins Ice Cream (featuring twenty-eight flavors) to learn they now carried only vanilla and chocolate ice cream, would that trouble you?

Now back to my original question: If future bird populations and species diversity plummeted to critically low levels, would you care? I think you should. Birds are truly good for the heart.

Heading Offshore

After several false starts, including prohibitive heavy fog and high seas, we took a whale watch cruise out of Bar Harbor in late July. The prospect of seeing bus-sized leviathans was appealing enough, but we were equally interested in the birds lurking offshore. In ecological terms, the deep pelagic zones might as well be a separate planet from the inshore waters. The seabirds and animals inhabiting these challenging realms are exquisitely designed to live and thrive way out there. In order to observe these intriguing creatures, we must enter their watery offshore domains.

With several hundred tourists boarding the 140-foot jet-powered catamaran, we headed directly for the bow of the vessel. The Atlanticat's captain made an announcement over the loud speaker: "There are three-to-five foot swells offshore." In truth, this capable multi-hulled vessel could easily manage those relatively minor sea conditions. Through power of suggestion, our captain may have influenced the psychological and gastrointestinal fates of some potential whale watchers by stating, "For passengers who don't have cast-iron stomachs, you may return to the dock and receive a ticket refund." Surprisingly, no ticket holders disembarked.

Soon we were racing across the open bay at thirty-plus knots! I sat next to an Iowa hog farmer and his wife on their first trip to Maine. As we encountered harbor porpoises and white-sided dolphins scrolling along the surface, I pointed out Wilson's storm petrels, tiny dark seabirds with white rumps that pattered the water surfaces as they fed.

Farther on, an occasional great shearwater scaled past the vessel. Then a gray-bodied sooty shearwater skittered into view, alternating its snappy, pumping flight with short graceful glides. Each summer, these birds visit Maine waters from the southern hemisphere, which was currently in its winter season. And, with wings folded back in pointed-arrow formation, northern gannets dived headlong into roiling schools of fish. Several Atlantic puffins buzzed past us, ferrying food to their puffling chicks in boroughs on Petit Manan Island.

The vessel slowed several times as we approached gigantic ocean sunfish, doggedly sculling their way across outer Frenchman's Bay. These ungainly fish can weigh more than a ton. Next we encountered a twenty-five-foot basking shark, a harmless, filter-feeding fish that swims and forages with its expansive mouth gaped wide open. Next a large blue shark swam into view.

After cruising at full speed for over an hour, we had reached a destination roughly thirty miles offshore, called "The Bumps." Normally, this was predictable whale territory, but we were finding no whales. The sea had calmed now, still and glassy as any country millpond.

Our captain opted for a zigzag course through the whale grounds, hoping to see a spout. Sizeable flocks of shearwaters and gulls loitered on the flat waters. A thick-bodied pomarine jaeger, a predatory, gull-like seabird, winged past us. Jaegers frequently pirate prey from other seabirds.

As we entered an area known as "The Ballpark," a humpback whale suddenly breached a hundred yards off the bow! The forty-five-foot whale launched itself upward, with only the tip of its tail touching the water. Showtime! This whale was well known to the boat crew as "Ark." Presumed to be thirty to forty years-old, he had been entangled in fishing gear a decade earlier. When rescuers finally freed him, Ark's dorsal fin carried a permanent notch in it.

Ark's next dive went deep, leaving behind only his "footprint" of dimpled water at the surface. He stayed down for several minutes, before resurfacing dramatically near our starboard rail. In true humpback fashion, he had blown bubbles to confuse and compress the swirling schools of fish from below. With his massive, sprawling jaws bulging with fish and tens of gallons of seawater, Ark's immense head rose fifteen feet above the waterline! On our return to shore, that Iowa farmer and I found plenty to talk about.

Hiding in the Woods

The summer nesting season holds many secrets and wonders. Most songbirds seek isolated woodland locations to build a nest and attempt a brood, while some, like eastern phoebes and American robins, are comfortable in closer proximity to humans.

By the sheerest chance, I encountered a ground-built nest during a morning outing. A smallish, olive-colored bird popped up practically beneath my feet, and landed mere feet away. Wobbling pathetically in an injured fashion and dragging one wing behind her, the bird began a broken-wing display to distract and lead me from her nest site. It was an ovenbird, a thrush-like warbler that builds a distinctive dome-shaped nest of grasses, leaves, mosses, and rootlets in shady, mixed woods. The bird's drab olive back color, spotted breast, and subtle orange-and-black head stripes help to camouflage her from predators.

I realized I must be standing very close to the nest. Without taking another step, I scanned the patchwork of leafy vegetation in the foreground. Amid the grassy motif of dead leaves, sticks, mosses, and ferns, I finally spotted the canted nest opening at ground level. Five creamy, speckled eggs lay inside. Even when I was standing almost above the nest, built by the female ovenbird in about five days, the camouflaged nest was virtually invisible.

I retreated temporarily, waiting until the parent ovenbird crept back to resume her incubating duties. After snapping a quick documentation photo, I vacated the premises.

Pitted against the tremendous odds and dangers of the natural world, we can only wish this secretive warbler a productive nesting season in Maine's summer woods. But what about her tropical wintering grounds? What are her prospects there? By October, ovenbirds travel to Mexico and the West Indies. Others will cross the Gulf waters and push southward to Panama and northern Venezuela. Those countries sound like secure wintering destinations, you might think.

Yes, but habitats are changing in dramatic ways in tropical regions, as mature forests are harvested for fuel and timber. Huge expanses are cleared for temporary, unsustainable agricultural projects and cattle grazing to supply cheap beef to U.S. fast-food chains. After a few seasons of use, the land often becomes nutrient-depleted, and is left to revert back to scrub growth.

The coffee producing industry exerts major influences on natural habitat conditions across Latin American countries. Most of the coffees that Americans consume (I drink two cups every morning) are of the sun-grown varieties. This farming method involves clearing of native forest land that formerly supported a trove of birds and other wildlife. For successful growth, these monocultures of sun-tolerant coffee rely on extensive application of herbicides, fungicides, pesticides, and chemical fertilizers. As such, these plantations are largely devoid of birds.

By contrast, shade-grown coffee varieties are planted beneath canopies of natural forest, where minimal pesticide use and chemical measures are required. In one comparative bird study near the Mexican/Guatemalan border, 184 bird species, 46 being migratory, were recorded in traditional shade-coffee plantations. As few as 6 to 12 species were recorded among adjacent full-sun monocultures.

We can all help to preserve migratory birds through our personal marketing choices. Buying shade-grown coffee is one easy and obvious way. Look for the Bird Friendly seal of the Smithsonian Migratory Bird Center. Go online for more information about how and where to purchase bird-friendly coffees, or ask local merchants to stock these brands. That nested ovenbird I discovered will never know of our choice of coffees, but she will benefit directly from our informed actions and market decisions to preserve critical habitat for her and hundreds of other bird species.

Maine's Fish Crows

Most everyone is familiar with crows. The customary crows we see in Maine are American crows. Anyhow, a crow is simply a crow, right? Well, the answer to that question depends on what part of Maine you are talking about. In recent years, the city of Rockland has hosted a different species of crow along its shoreline neighborhoods—a small congregation of fish crows. Fish crows are a scaled-down version of their larger American crow cousins, with shorter legs, more pointed, swept-back wings, and a slimmer bill.

The fish crow also has a shorter neck, and tends to puff out its throat feathers and hunch forward while vocalizing. Its choppy wingbeats are relatively rapid, with occasional bouts of hyperkinetic, mid-air spins interspersed with sputtering pauses. Despite the species' proportionally longer, slightly fan-shaped tail, these diminutive crows can easily pass our notice.

Like a number of other southern-based species, fish crows have crept northward in recent decades. First documented in Maine in 1978, fish crows moved up through river systems of the Mississippi Valley, and are now found inland to Waterville and Bangor. They have nested in scattered numbers in Brunswick and around Portland's Evergreen Cemetery since the early 1980s, and have occurred along the Kennebec River in Richmond.

As their name implies, these crows are often found along coastal shorelines and riverbanks where they forage for fish and crustaceans in shallow water. They are equally at home in manure-strewn farm fields, where they garner insects, seeds, and berries. Like other crow species, they are "generalists" that will ingest most any edible items that come their way. In urban settings, they are consummate dumpster divers around fast food restaurants.

Now nesting in Rockland, fish crows have also been recorded on multiple Thomaston-Rockland Christmas Birds Counts. In the summer of 2018, I documented breeding activity in stands of mature white pines at a Rockland locality. At least three pairs of fish crows signaled their active breeding status through mutual feather preening (a.k.a. allopreening), paired aerial maneuvers, and carrying nesting sticks into the pine canopies. A few weeks later, their vocal fledgling offspring were being fed by parents.

The easiest and most reliable way to identify these smallish crows is by their distinctive high-pitched voices. While American crows produce the familiar flat "caw, caw" sounds, the fish crow's calls have a thin, nasal quality that sounds, to my ear, like a statement of denial. What do I mean by that? If we could possibly inquire of a fish crow, "Are you an ordinary American crow?" the fish crow would deny it: "Uh-uh; Uh-uh," with an accented first syllable.

Just for fun one day, I improvised my best fish crow impression, energetically uttering "uh-uh; uh-uh; uh-uh" calls along Rockland's Summer Street. To my delight, several of the crows quickly circled overhead in shrill, scolding tones! One can only imagine what passersby might have thought: "Did you see that guy staring up into the sky and making those strange noises?" It goes without saying that every coastal crow now deserves second and closer looks.

MEGU Equals Mew Gull

Some people seek rainbows in pursuit of beauty or inspiration. Me, I have an odd practice of scanning parking lots to see what forms of bird life might occupy such sparse, open spaces. Like finding the proverbial pot of gold at rainbow's end, I have been richly rewarded on several occasions.

Around 6 a.m. one August morning, I pulled into the parking area behind Thomaston Grocery, where sixty to seventy ring-billed gulls loitered and preened themselves on the feather-strewn tarmac. Because August is the prime period for feather molt in gulls, the scene there resembled an overnight pillow fight carried to extremes.

Depending on the vagaries of daily tide cycles and fluctuating weather, this parking area hosts a slate of morning gulls. Among its usual congregations of herring and black-backed gulls, the current inhabitants included two marked ring-billed gulls, wearing numbered orange wing tags from a Massachusetts gull study.

At the rear of the lot, five gulls splashed in a bathtub-sized rain puddle. "All ringed-bills," I reckoned. The adult ringed-billed is medium-sized, gray-backed gull, with yellowish legs and a dark-banded straw-yellow bill. Then I noticed a slightly smaller and more compact looking gull. Its back feathers appeared a tad darker than the surrounding birds.

Edging my vehicle closer to the assembled throng, my suspicions rose about the darker gull's identity, as my pulse consecutively quickened. Further investigation revealed a short, straight yellow bill with no bill-band. In contrast to the other gulls, the rounded head profile gave this bird a rather gentle expression. (Yes, certain gull species exhibit a continuum of perceived "facial expressions" that are mildly useful with identifications.) The gull's eyes were dark colored, resembling two coffee beans suspended against a white background.

    I could no longer suppress a developing conclusion: after years of gawking around parking lots and beachfronts, I had stumbled upon a mew gull! The gull's wing feathers and coverts were badly worn, leaving a fuzzy patch of white on its lower back. It appeared to be a molting sub-adult. There was now little doubt in my mind of its true identity. At the time, this individual represented only the third state record for mew gull in Maine. Its early arrival date on the U.S. East Coast was also unusual. Three of the four subspecies within the mew gull complex exist across expanses of Alaska, northwest Canada, and Siberia. Their look-alike European counterpart, the common gull, occasionally strays into Newfoundland in late summer and fall.

I reported the sighting to the Maine-Birds website, and scores of birders came to observe and photograph the gull in the following two weeks. The gull's favored hangouts included school rooftops and adjacent recreational fields. During low tides, it left there to forage in the nearby mudflats.

Beyond the obvious rarity of the gull, we were still puzzling over its geographic and precise subspecies origins. Gulls are chronic wanderers that can show up in odd places hundreds or thousands of miles from home. Given the species' world ranges and distribution patterns, the Thomaston mew gull must have trekked three thousand miles or more, regardless of its geographical origins.

Through the marvels of the internet, I forwarded some querying photos to gull experts in Newfoundland and England. No quick or definitive answers came. Although this globe-trotting creature had not flown beyond the rainbow's bend, it certainly flew far enough to make my birding day!

Venturing for Vultures

For folks in the midcoast region, summer sightings of turkey vultures are common, but that wasn't always the case. When ornithologist Ralph Palmer published his *Maine Birds* in 1949, he cited just twelve records over the period of 1862 to 1944. In the intervening seventy years, things have changed dramatically across New England. Eventually, turkey vultures were confirmed as Maine breeders at Camden's Bald Mountain in 1982. But do vultures currently nest around Knox and Lincoln Counties? Two decades ago, I had encountered a successful vulture pair with two fledglings amid the wreckage of a collapsing summer cottage in Owls Head.

During the inaugural phase of the five-year Maine Bird Atlas project, I struggled to answer that question, without much success. Simple observations of soaring vultures do not translate to confirmed nesting status, though. My fascination with vultures is not new. Scientific experiments have revealed that turkey vultures possess an extraordinary sense of smell in locating carrion. Perhaps more surprisingly, they are somewhat discriminating in their dietary choices, showing a preference for defunct herbivores over carnivores. So, in theory, a roadkilled deer carcass would rate higher on the menu than a dead cat or coyote. And, contrary to popular misconception, fresher meat is preferred, when available.

In a parallel scientific quest of my own, I'd once tried to persuade my wife to recline (temporarily, mind you) in a grassy field where I might get photos of vulture landings. Her muttered response was less than scientific.

Last week, I ventured into a stand of mature red oak and white pine woods in Warren, where numbers of summer vultures roost overnight. Perhaps I'd find evidence of breeding activity there. Unlike the highly-visible nest of ospreys and eagles, vultures are highly secretive in selecting nest sites. Concealment from animal predators is of pressing concern, since the young are fed carrion that emits strong, telltale odors. For vultures, there is no formal nest building. Favored sites include precipitous cliffs, caves, hollow stumps and logs, and dense shrubbery. For these reasons, nest detections by humans are understandably low.

The sun-dappled floor of the Warren grove was thoroughly whitewashed with excrement and dozens of large molted wing and body feathers. Adult vultures molt portions of feathers throughout the summer, while supplies of carrion are readily acquired. As I explored the grove, one sizeable ground cavity under an immense fallen oak trunk caught my attention. Despite the prospect of promise, it was unutilized for nesting. That site bears checking in the future.

With their featherless reddish head and heavy bill, vultures are eminently equipped to perform nature's clean-up tasks. I believe vultures get an undeservedly bad rap as disgusting, filthy creatures, capable of spreading disease. Actually, the reverse is true. With their impressively robust digestive systems and cast-iron stomachs, they can ingest strains of germs and bacteria that would likely sicken or kill humans. The vulture stomach can effectively process and sterilize toxins and anthrax spores without ill effects to the bird.

By removing vast quantities of decaying meat from the environment, vultures reduce contamination of air and groundwater. It is documented that vultures habitually defecate on their own feet and legs. What is the basis of this unsavory behavior, you ask? One possible benefit is to cool their legs in extreme hot weather (birds don't sweat to cool off). Secondly, the birds can disinfect their own legs, after contact with bacteria-laden carcasses on the ground. Amazing, but true, vulture excrement is totally sterile!

Juvenile vultures eventually join the ranks of adults at fall roosts, before sailing southward for winter. In the meantime, I'm left to ponder those gray-headed juvenile birds. Were they reared somewhere in the Warren zip code?

Summering with Vultures

In 2018, I wrote a column on turkey vultures, describing my unsuccessful efforts to confirm nesting vultures in Maine, in conjunction with the statewide, five-year Maine Bird Atlas Project. I'm relieved to report that the 2019 season produced a major turnabout, when a local land owner informed me of a perennial vulture nesting site on her property. On May 12, 2019, I made an initial stop at the secluded nest grove. Brief, weekly follow-ups continued through most of the summer, and at closer intervals as the mid-August fledging dates approached. My intent was to document progress at the nest, while limiting stress on the parents and the developing nestlings as much as possible. I accomplished this by pre-adjusting camera settings prior to arrival times and keeping site visits down to a few minutes.

Using the term loosely, the nest itself was housed inside a complex of ledged rock formations, bisected by a narrow cleft that allowed parental access through the roof of the grotto entrance. Two sizeable eggs, creamy-white with lavender-brown spots and splotches, lay together on a mantle of bare red-oak leaves. A mossy, lichen-covered shelf of overhanging granite provided shade and basic protection from the elements. Within such cave environments, hot summer temperatures are generally eleven to thirteen degrees Fahrenheit cooler than ambient outside conditions.

For such impressively bulky individuals, turkey vultures are rather timid and secretive by nature. They do not build a nest as such. Instead, caves and cliff banks, hollow stumps, dense shrubbery, and unused buildings are commonly utilized. Meticulous concealment from predators is essential due to the pungent odors of carrion being fed to young. In contrast with nest-building species that transport nest materials with their bills (most songbirds) or feet (raptors), vultures fit neither transit category. The vulture's large, flat feet are relatively weak, and its bill is unsuited for these fussy tasks.

Incubation of eggs requires between thirty to forty-five days, as both parents share in those responsibilities. On my June 22 visit, two white downy chicks were huddling beneath the thick armor of rock. The chicks were largely immobile at that early stage, but both birds puffed their feathers and elevated their downy heads to appear as fearsome and intimidating as possible. Both opened their bills and hissed defensively. Lacking a syrinx, the muscular song-producing organ of songbirds, vultures produce only hissing and grunting sounds.

Between intervals of my regular weekly checks, the chicks grew rapidly. By June 29, dark pin feathers had emerged along the outer wing margins. By the July 15 visit, their lengthening wings were sheathed with blackish covert feathers, still framed in fine, white down. Feather development does not occur randomly, as emerging feathers grow in specific patterns or rows called "feather tracts." The process might be likened to penciling-in a trace-the-dots puzzle image. A full set of flight feathers was evident by July 20.

July 27 was a red letter day for a couple of reasons! The chicks were now asserting signs of independence from the squeeze of their grotto confines, as the pair stood on the granite shelf above the nest cave. Most of their dark-brown upper body feathers had emerged, and bourgeoning tails had grown to about half-length. Their downy collar and breast remained white, while their eyes retained a medium-blue tint from the hatching period. One chick made a leisurely retreat back inside the cave, while the second bird eyed me with cautious conjecture. I noted the bird's rimmed, over-sized nostrils. As scavengers, turkey vultures locate food by smell as well as sight. We see them rocking high in the air, scanning for available carrion. At other times, vultures cruise the lower heights, as they quarter into the wind, sniffing at treetop level to detect a meal. Decaying flesh emits a putrid-smelling gas called *mercaptan* that alerts vultures to the presence of nearby carrion. Mercaptan is also added to commercial propane products to help detect gas leaks. It is a key component of bad breath and flatulence in humans, as well.

    Something else was markedly different on this occasion though. For the first time during our summer acquaintance, the vultures did not hiss at me! They eyed me with wise caution, but remained calm and silent. I speculated about their change of behavior. Considering our multiple face-to-face contacts, had the pair grown accustomed to seeing me? That same fellow that emerged occasionally, peering into their inner sanctum? The same one that didn't stay long, didn't harm or threaten them, and quietly left the premises shortly thereafter? An acquired sense of familiarity? you ask. Perhaps so, but possibly there was more to it. On previous visits, I'd stationed myself directly above them to capture the interior nest photos. Birds feel uneasy when a potential predator is positioned over them. Now, their self-determined ledge position placed them safely above me. They never hissed again.

    An August 3 visit provided momentum in gaining the pair's acceptance and trust. By this point, they were spending daytimes outside the cave. It was eighty-six degrees Fahrenheit when I arrived at mid-day, and the vultures had sought the shady comfort of the leafy oak grove. They paced tentatively before stepping out of sight behind a rock. Within a minute, one bird returned to full view and settled itself confidently atop the bare ledge, some sixty feet away. Fully aware of our mutual presences, we made eye contact. Wow, the bird's eye color had transitioned from blue to a warm brown. We gauged each other for a good ten minutes.

In the following week, I witnessed other shifts in behavior, as the chicks gradually strayed farther from the nest. They were flying by August 9, making short hops between forest openings, apparently to where the adults could readily spot them from the air to deliver food. Unlike most other land birds, vultures do not transport food with their bills or feet. Instead, food is stored temporarily in the crop, an expanded muscular pouch in the gullet that is part of their digestive system. At feeding, adults regurgitate the stored food morsels down the throats of dependent young.

Realizing that the rapidly-maturing birds would soon fledge, I revisited on August 11 to find the pair nestled at the edge of an adjacent blueberry barren just outside the woods. The following day, I found them perched near the nest on a stout diagonal tree limb, that doubled as a roost and feeding perch. The vultures were full-sized and feathered now, and, except for the grayish head and dark bill of the juvenile, they resembled adults.

On August 14, I had a final, and very enlightening, encounter. As one juvenile sat on the feeding perch, an adult vulture landed in a nearby pine top. I wondered how the juvenile would react. Obviously aware and stimulated by the adult's arrival, the juvenile leaned forward to eject a huge pellet onto the ground. Pellets contain indigestible or uneaten food matter coughed up prior to a next meal. This action typically occurs every day or two, but the anticipation of receiving the food offering may have instigated the pellet cast. When I later inspected the pellet, it contained scraps of juicy, red meat, with legions of bottle flies and beetles sharing in the feast.

Studies have shown that, contrary to popular perceptions that vultures seek out putrid or rotten meat, they prefer fresher sources when available. The vulture's ultra-strong stomach acids also afford it protection against powerful bacterial forms, including anthrax, that would sicken or kill humans. And although it sounds counter-intuitive, the vulture's fecal output is entirely sterile.

My intriguing summer season with a vulture family ended in mid-August. In late October, I noticed a vulture riding the fall winds. I pondered where it had nested and where it would travel next.

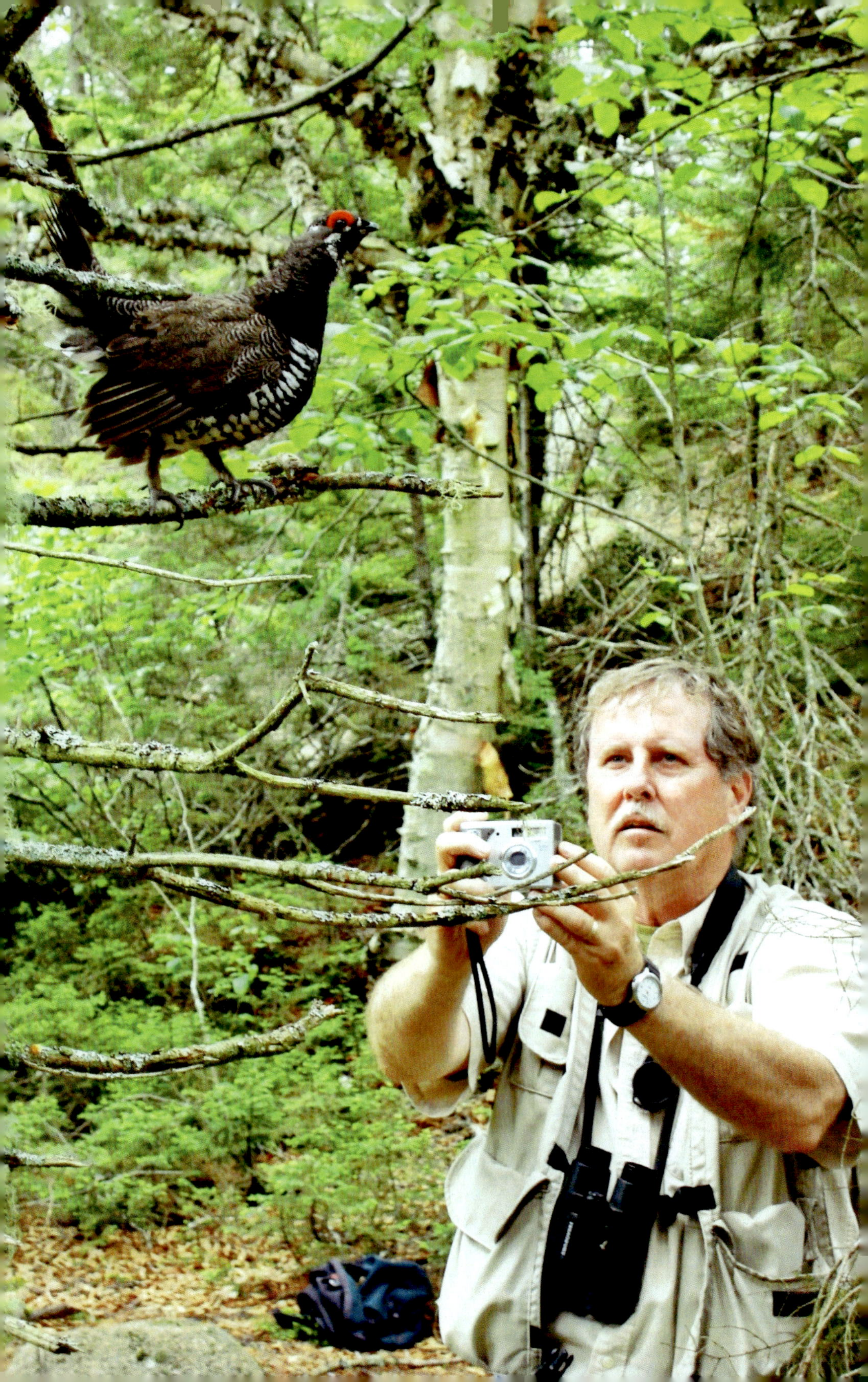

Two Grouse

Two members of the gallinaceous or "chicken-like" grouse family occur in Maine. Despite some variations in coloring and feather patterns, the ruffed grouse and spruce grouse are similar in shape and size, but their contrasting behavioral tendencies are quite dissimilar. Both species occupy specialized habitats that meet their essential life needs.

Throughout the state, the more familiar ruffed grouse predominates. A favored Maine game bird, hunters annually harvest about a half-million of these grouse. The vast majority of ruffed grouse have a black tail band and a black ruff of feathers around the neck. Several color phases, ranging from gray to red, occur, but the grayer forms are more common in our northern latitudes. In fall, there are instances of grouse mortalities as birds occasionally get a bit tipsy on fermented berries and collide with windows and other fixed objects. Under winter snow conditions, ruffed grouse often feed high off the ground, seeking tree buds, fruits, and berries. By September, projections called *pectinations* begin growing on the sides of their toes. These fleshy nubs, which fall off in spring, help grouse walk in a snowshoe fashion over deep snow cover, and provide extra grip on icy branches. During severe winter cold or storm conditions, grouse will burrow into insulating snow banks at night.

Despite an occasional tame or pokey individual, ruffed grouse are vigilant birds that readily flush when disturbed. Anyone who has experienced a woodland grouse exploding into flight beneath their feet knows of what I speak. In an alternate manner, a ruffed grouse may perk up its head like a domestic chicken, to extend its neck forward and scamper toward protective cover.

An amazingly confiding species, the spruce grouse is a true boreal forest specialist. During Lewis and Clark's 1804-06 western expedition, Meriwether Lewis described the species as "gentle," which may be why it's often referred to as "fool hen." They're found in northern coniferous forest habitats from Alaska to Maine, and our state has arguably the largest distribution and abundance of spruce grouse.

The male's black chest and dark gray/brown plumage is speckled with white barring, and his arching red eye combs add a dramatic flair to an otherwise inconspicuous presence. When approached, the halting spruce grouse relies on cryptic camouflage to avoid detection. Sometimes they may crouch or run short distances, only to take refuge in a nearby tree. As the most arboreal of the grouse, they are well adapted to perching and moving about in trees.

The spruce grouse diet changes with the seasons. Consisting mainly of pine and spruce needles in winter, the diet in summer includes berries, succulent leaves, and insects. To accommodate the stringent winter diet of tough needles, the gizzard size increases by seventy-five percent, and the digestive tract increases in length. Spruce grouse and ruffed grouse can and do occur in the same habitats, but there is no open hunting season for spruce grouse anywhere in Maine.

Voices from the Woods

Around 4:30 each June morning, I anticipate a resident male cardinal and a certain chirping robin in my yard, as they launch their pre-dawn songs. A resourceful blue jay imitates the two-syllabled whistles of the broad-winged hawk pair that nests in a nearby oak grove. In theory, by imitating the call of an imminent predator, the jay clears away competing birds from my seed feeders.

As we enter the final days of June, nesters have established territorial footholds in local woods and backyards. In following weeks, the old maxim "what you see is what you get" applies aptly to the Maine birding scene. Barring predator attacks or catastrophic weather events, June through July is a predictably stable period for most nesting birds.

Song-wise, some musical characteristics have changed slightly as the season has progressed. Some warblers have altered their May song-types, gradually switching from intense, accented songs to more sedate, scaled-down renditions.

Of the eight species of warblers nesting within earshot of my back deck, the male chestnut-sided warbler is a good case in point. Upon his mid-May arrival, this bird's vocal offerings are focused on advertising and establishing his territory. His emphatic "pleased, pleased, pleased to MEETCHA!" message proclaimed his breeding eligibility to prospective mates. By late June, he often uses a toned-down, loose trill to maintain territorial contact with his nesting companion.

By contrast, the male black-and-white warbler's thin, squeaky-wheel song varies little with the seasons. His habitual pursuit of larvae and live insects along large branches and tree trunks also persists into summer. Creeping up and down and probing bark crevices with his pick-like bill, this warbler's behavior is more reminiscent of a nuthatch. Despite their devotedness to trunk surfaces, black and whites nest on the ground near the base of a tree, stump or rock.

Another ground-nesting warbler of the deciduous forest, the ovenbird issues his ringing "teacher, teacher, teacher!" song from a mid-level perch. This warbler's song actually rises in volume and intensity at the end. Methodically, his body bobs along horizontal branches, treading as if his feet were somehow stuck in glue. The female ovenbird constructs her well-concealed, dome-shaped nest in a depression of dead leaves, lining it with grasses, plant fibers, and rootlets. Shaped like an old-fashioned oven, the nest is practically invisible from above.

Several American redstarts inhabit the second growth woods behind my house. Redstarts are renowned for their showy, active behavior, flashing the yellow or orange patches on their sides, wings, and tails, during courtship and daily foraging activities.

The yellow-toned female redstart typically constructs a cup-like nest within about a week's time. One unusual nest was reportedly built in less than three days, representing 650 to 700 trips to the site with construction materials in tow.

The adult male redstart's distinctive black-and-orange plumage makes them hard to mistake for other warblers. However, it's always worth checking individual birds that don't quite match those perfect images in your bird guide. Hearing a redstart singing close by, I spotted what first appeared to be a yellow-patterned female.

With closer observation, I learned that the redstart in question wasn't a female at all. It was a young male, a hatchling from the previous year that had acquired his partial adult plumage. Its gray head and a few emerging black feathers around the face, throat, and chest were conclusive evidence. As with most warblers, full-adult plumage is achieved in the second year of life.

Be listening for the bird voices in your woods. You might be surprised by who's out there.

Exploring the Rockland Bog

In mid-June I trekked into the Rockland Bog (a.k.a. Oyster River Bog) to peruse the unique array of plants and animal life found within its spongy, mired interior.

The word *bog* is of Gaelic origin, coming from *bogach,* a derivative of the adjective "soft." With peat deposits ranging from ten to twenty feet in depth, the majority of true bog territory lies within Rockland boundaries in a general area between Dodge Mountain and Meadow Mountain. Although the bog is located relatively close to civilization, it provides a genuine sense of remoteness and timelessness that is hard to duplicate in most other settings.

During the last Ice Age, about ten thousand years ago, pressurized glacial action gouged shallow depressions or basins out of the bedrock. As the glaciers receded, pockets were created in the landscape, as the land eventually decompressed and ascended upward. The floor of the bog is still lined with telltale marine clay deposits, however. Hemmed-in by its own gently sloping sides, the six hundred-acre bog is an immense living terrarium on a grand scale.

Advancing toward the open bog, several transitional zones of plant and animal communities become apparent. The upland hardwood sections are home to a variety of wood warblers, including American redstarts, myrtle, and black-and-white warblers.

Next we pass through sections of white pine that eventually give way to flooded maple swamp. Farther on, velvet-needled tamaracks and wiry black spruces predominant the scene. In these inner sections, the ground becomes lush with delicate, chest-high ferns, and the omnipresent sphagnum mosses that carpet the bog's platform of life. Here we find Nashville warblers, Canada warblers, and a relatively uncommon breeder in these parts: the yellow-bellied flycatcher that occupies primarily wet, shaded woods. From within the green, walled underbrush, black-masked common yellowthroat warblers trill their *"witchety, witchety"* song.

And finally reaching the open bog itself, we find a quaking mossy mat of cranberry vines, carnivorous pitcher plants and sundews, clumps of white cotton grasses, and stunning upright clusters of Arethusa (dragon-mouth) orchids. Some rutted, perimeter game trails meander along thick tangles of leatherleaf and bog laurel. A several-acre-sized acidic pond at the central bog is speckled with budded yellow pond lilies. At pond's edge, squealing hen wood ducks often lead their downy broods safely from sight.

The highly specialized bog habitat is ill-suited for the majority of Maine's nesting songbirds. To the energetic, tail-pumping palm warbler, however, it's an ideal setting to raise a clutch. Palm warblers winter in the southeastern U.S., where they reportedly show some limited utilization of their namesake palm tree habitats. These are early spring migrants, arriving by mid-April and remaining into the chill of October.

Palm warblers nest on or near the ground, where the female builds a nest of fine grasses. Their bog-built nests are partially buried in the moss. In favorable habitats, such as the bog, several pairs may nest in tight proximity. Of two subspecies of palm warblers, the brighter eastern population is characterized by yellowish underparts, olive backs and solid chestnut caps. Their subspecies western counterparts are paler, with a whitish belly.

Weskeag Sparrows

To some folks, sparrows are merely an afterthought, as those "little brown jobs" that inhabit our neighborhoods, yards, and trails. The ubiquitous song sparrow nests in a variety of habitat types across the entire continent. Song sparrows are generalists, meaning they can readily adapt to conditions within diverse environments. As such, song sparrows and American robins are contenders as our most plentiful songbirds.

South Thomaston's Weskeag Marsh has lots of sparrows, too. Listed among Maine's twenty-two Important Bird Areas (IBAs), Weskeag provides unique or specialized habitats that are vital to bird breeding, wintering, and migration routines. In particular, Weskeag provides essential grassland and salt marsh habitats for several species with restrictive nesting requirements.

New England's grassland areas have declined precipitously in recent decades. And related factors, such as reforestation and intensification of agricultural practices, have contributed to the current declines in northern harrier, eastern meadowlark, and bobolink populations.

Grassland conservation is one important reason why Weskeag merits its IBA designation. Maine Fish & Wildlife manages acres of the upland fields that support those nesting eastern meadowlarks and bobolinks. The small, streaky savannah sparrow does well in grassy upland sectors. Savannahs are short-tailed, with crisp streaking to mid-belly and a variable yellow stripe above the eye. Not particularly shy, they will perch openly on weed stalks or fence wires, and chip aggressively whenever their nest is approached by intruders.

Two outlier species of sharp-tailed sparrows, the Nelson's and saltmarsh sparrows, have specific habitat needs linked to their marine environment. Found along Weskeag River's ditches and dike terrain, their namesake "sharp-tailed" appearance is due to spiky, pointed tail feathers. Of the two closely-related species, the Nelson's is far more numerous in the midcoast. These skulky sprites can pass unnoticed unless one hears their dry, trilled songs, sounding like a pressurized escape of steam.

With limited populations of the threatened saltmarsh sparrows in particular, Weskeag may well be their northern-most outpost for successful breeding. The saltmarsh species has an unusual mating system for a songbird, with males simply roving about, seeking females, rather than choosing a defined nesting territory. The males take no part in caring for the eggs or young. A species of special conservation concern, saltmarsh sparrows are rapidly disappearing from the eastern United States. Twenty years ago, their population was estimated at more than 250,000. Today those numbers have plummeted to less than one-fifth of that total, and continue to drop by 9 percent a year.

Aside from obvious habitat losses, their growing survival challenges involve elevated tidal levels that disrupt nesting activity. Nests are usually placed just above the average high-tide mark, but some nests are destroyed by the frequently occurring extreme tides. Here's the rub: The birds' nesting-cycle lasts twenty-three to twenty-four days—just a few days less than the twenty-eight-day tidal cycles influenced by the moon's gravitational pull. If flooding only happens every twenty-eight days or so, then the sparrows can just about fit their nesting cycles between two sets of extreme tides. If flooding events become more frequent, however, the egg-laying window collapses; eggs either float away or the (altricial) chicks drown. Although eggs may withstand a brief wetting in seawater, the nest is doomed if tidal water levels rise over the nest rim. With ocean levels rising between two and six millimeters each year, the saltmarsh species could become extinct by 2050.

What's a Piscivore?

When carnivorous animals are mentioned, we might visualize a charging grizzly bear or prowling lion. By any definition, these are clearly animals that feed on flesh. Other assorted species, including most humans, fit this category to some extent. If we chronicled the carnivorous birds, eagles and great horned owls would rank high on that list. How about American robins? Are those sedate, demure birds possible contenders for a carnivore's Who's Who list? I think they qualify, since the bulk of the summer robin's diet consists of plump and meaty earthworms. Wintering robins eventually become obligate vegetarians, feeding on waste fruits and berries once the ground freezes.

Carnivorous birds can be classified several ways, depending on specific aspects of their diets. Let's briefly review these. *Insectivores* include flycatchers, warblers, and swallows that consume mostly flying and crawling insects. *Avivores* are the bird-eating raptors, like the sharp-shinned hawks that patrol your bird feeders, and swift, open-sky aerialists like peregrine falcons. *Molluscivores* are mollusk-eating birds with specialized physical traits. Common eiders and American oystercatchers can process a shellfish diet. Relying on their strong, muscular gizzards to grind the shells, sea ducks ingest whole blue mussels. Oystercatchers pry apart hardened mollusk shells with their stout, chiseled bills, fashioned in the handy shape of a customized shucking tool.

And we mustn't ignore the *piscivores*, those birds that rely primarily on fish for sustenance. This group has specialized bill structures, and includes puffins, loons, cormorants, herons, egrets, and ospreys. Slippery fish are either speared directly by a sharp-pointed bill or corralled into bills equipped with ridged edges, like those of merganser ducks and Atlantic puffins. Some species have sensitized bills, containing fine nerve endings that detect a fish, even when prey is not directly seen.

Fish eaters have other anatomical adaptations that boost hunting success, such as scaly feet and strong talons. The long, thin legs of wading egrets and herons afford a stealthy hunting approach in watery habitats. Counter-shaded plumage on the great blue heron provides camouflage while stalking water prey. Feet set farther back on the bodies of puffins, loons, and cormorants provide sustaining propulsion for efficient, underwater maneuvers. Tapered, flipper-styled wings enable species such as long-tailed ducks to pursue prey in rapid, twisting "flight" under water. Depending on the bird species and the size of its prey, fish may be swallowed whole or ripped into pieces for convenient consumption.

Ospreys and northern gannets make spectacular, precipitous dives to seize fish from beneath the surface. The skulls of both species are equipped with protective air sacs to minimize the cranial shocks of striking water surfaces at thirty miles per hour. On a lesser scale, belted kingfisher pairs at Weskeag Marsh hover and plunge-dive into swirling schools of small fish in the shallow pools. At other times, the fisher pair waits patiently atop roadside perches to assess fish stocks and target potential prey.

It may sound like a stretch to label any sparrow species as a fish eater, but my experiences with Nelson's sparrows at Weskeag prove otherwise. During a super high-tide event, schools of tiny fish had filtered beyond the grassy margins of the overflowing salt pannes. The flooded grasses were literally brimming with flipping fish, and a few had grounded themselves. Soon a begging juvenile sharp-tailed sparrow rushed along the wet ground, where it was joined by an adult carrying a wriggling fish in its bill. The adult promptly shoved the fish down the chick's open gullet. It was a tight fit, for sure, but a nourishing meal for the chick.

Whip-poor-wills

As a child, I heard the haunting nighttime calls of distant whip-poor-wills that penetrated my opened bedroom windows. Those melancholy sounds filled my mind, and came to signify a Maine summer. With the passage of years, those sounds have gradually ceased in much of coastal and eastern Maine, as whip-poor-will populations have plummeted by 90 percent in some parts of the bird's overall range. Two members of the nightjar family, whip-poor-will and common nighthawk, nest in Maine, while seven other nightjar species inhabit North America.

One July night, I undertook a Maine Audubon citizen-science study of whip-poor-wills and common nighthawks (a species that is unrelated to actual hawks) in an effort to document the status of these diminishing birds. I enjoy any detective challenge that involves some sleuthing around the natural world. But since I hadn't heard a whip-poor-will's call in perhaps twenty years, I approached the survey with mild skepticism of success.

A mottled, brown bird with cryptic patterning, whip-poor-wills measure about nine inches in length. Being crepuscular creatures, they are most active at dawn and dusk. Their large red eyes help whip-poor-wills locate night-cruising insects, such as moths, beetles, and mosquitoes. The bill is relatively small, belying the bird's enormous gaping yaw that can accommodate sizeable prey.

Embracing similar protocols to the Maine Owl Monitoring Program, the nightjar study consisted of stopping and listening for six-minute stints at ten pre-determined sites located at least one mile apart. I chose particular stops based on suitable habitat characteristics: For whip-poor-wills that means dry, pine barrens or semi-dry deciduous and mixed woods with open spaces or fields nearby. Safe roadside areas for parking after dark were another consideration. Whip-poor-wills are most vocal on bright moonlit nights, and their breeding is synchronized with the lunar cycles, so that young hatch before a full moon. Two eggs are laid directly on the ground and are occasionally moved short distances to shadier spots by the female.

So how did my survey efforts fare? At 9:30 p.m. a beaming full moon, at 99.4 percent of illumination capacity, lit surrounding fields and woods. A haze of courting fireflies signaled to potential mates above tall field grasses, as each of several races of fireflies blinked in their prescribed frequencies and occupied marginally different altitudes.

Listening conditions were superior—not a stir of breeze or wind. Nevertheless, I heard no nightjars at any of my ten stops. But, otherwise, the night was a veritable smorgasbord of intriguing sounds. Several woodcocks twittered overhead, and a yapping red fox, mooing cow, and several rounds of home-launched fireworks enlivened the atmosphere. At one stop, a stately buck deer stood fixed and staring at me from a chest-deep hayfield. The buck blew and snorted deliberately and then stomped a few yards away. When I randomly snorted back at him, he inched closer to inspect me.

If you spend summer evenings near water in Maine, you will discover an auditory reality: amphibians rule the nocturnal soundscapes. Near the end of my survey route, I paused at the edge of a cattail swamp. A thrum of exuberant frogs sang heartily in natural, three-part harmonies. Armies of clunking green frogs carried the main melody line, with dozens of bullfrogs adding a deep, throbbing bass. Lofts of gray tree frogs sang the tenor notes from twenty feet in the air. Not to be outdone, two dialoging marsh wrens chittered and sputtered from the reeds.

Please take a few minutes to stand outdoors on some quiet summer evening and just listen. I hope you get to hear a whip-poor-will. I hope that future generations will get to hear one.

PART III

Moving into Fall

A Visit from Big Bird

From years of birding and amateur photography, I've accumulated catalogues of photos for my bi-monthly bird articles. Nevertheless, I prefer to write about the most recent scenarios and use timely photos, whenever possible.

An interesting scenario began on September 9, 2013, when I received some online photos of a mammoth white bird taken by lady on Wheeler's Bay in St. George. While boating in the bay, she photographed the bird and forwarded her photos to me. The bird in question was an American white pelican!

The following morning, I investigated the scene. Bingo! From the outlook at Marina Road near Clark's Island, I found the pelican standing stoically on a ledge of seaweed some fifty yards from shore, with bill partially tucked into its feathers. Suddenly the sword-like, orange bill was revealed, as the bird yawned widely, billowing its fleshy throat pouch skyward, like a windblown glob of bubble gum. Pelicans stretch their throat frequently to keep the skin supple.

Standing at four-feet tall, with an impressive nine-foot wingspan, and weighing sixteen to forty pounds, the American white pelican is one of North America's largest birds. White pelicans breed mainly on isolated islands in freshwater lakes in the northern Great Plains and the mountain West. During the nonbreeding season, they favor shallow coastal bays, inlets, and estuaries along the Gulf Coast region.

White pelicans are powerful, graceful fliers that travel in V-shaped flock formations. With their long, plank-like wings, pelicans soar effortlessly on warm, elevating thermals. Thermals are used in different ways, depending on specific distances. With foraging areas frequently located thirty miles or more from the nest colonies, commuting flights occur at the lower and mid-thermal levels. The upper reaches of thermal columns are reserved for cross-country flights.

White pelicans differ from the smaller, oceanic brown pelicans. They do not plunge-dive to capture prey, but work in cooperative groups to corral fish and amphibians living just below the water's surface. With each fish-eating catch, the gaping bill also gathers about two gallons of water.

Breeding colonies may contain hundreds of birds. With the exception of size differences (males are larger), the sexes are similar. During the spring nesting season, these birds grow a distinctive, plate-like knob on the upper mandible that is shed shortly after the egg-laying.

While unusual in these parts, white pelicans visit midcoast waters on occasion. A flock of five or six such birds appeared at nearby Spruce Head two years before, following a strong southerly ocean storm. And a single white pelican spent several weeks at Lake Josephine and adjacent northern farm fields in Aroostook County.

For half an hour, the St. George pelican preened its shaggy head, stretched its wings and napped. Then, with a labored whumpf, whumpf, whumpf of wing flaps, the giant bird launched itself from the ledge top, landing out in mid-bay. It would eventually return south, but Maine birders enjoyed a live visit from Big Bird himself.

Bronzed Cowbird

Late October 2010 turned out to be an auspicious time for Oregon research ornithologist Randy Moore to visit with family in Rockland. Looking out the window one morning at his mother's house, he observed lively flocks of migrating sparrows and blackbirds eating seeds scattered on the ground outside. Among the busy troupes of birds, Randy spotted a Lincoln's sparrow and then a rusty blackbird among the scavenging flocks. "That's very cool," he thought. Then a stocky, thick-necked blackbird caught his attention. The bird showed a heavy, conical bill and a slight ruff of feathers around its nape. This atypical blackbird also had coral-red eyes. Next he noticed the bird's iridescent blue flight feathers, in sharp contrast to the otherwise flat black plumage.

As an experienced birder and trained field observer, Randy concluded that the bird in question must be a male bronzed cowbird! But what was it doing this far north in Maine? Previously known as red-eyed cowbirds, bronzed cowbirds nest in limited ranges of coastal Louisiana, lower Texas, Arizona, and New Mexico. The main core of their breeding range extends from Mexico into Central America.

Randy contacted Chris Bartlett, a member of the Maine Bird Records Committee, who confirmed that the bronzed cowbird species had never been documented anywhere in the New England region. In these days of instant communication links, news of such accidental avian rarities spreads rapidly throughout the pipelines of the birding internet. The announcement of this vagrant species would likely attract a number of birding enthusiasts to the scene. In some cases, residential neighborhoods can be inundated by hordes of birders hoping to sight a rarity. Several residents around the Rockland cowbird's immediate vicinity were informed that parties of "nutty, but otherwise harmless," birders could soon arrive.

Readers will be more familiar with the brown-headed cowbird pairs that summer in New England. By size comparison, the male brown-headed cowbird is slightly smaller than his bronzed cousin, with a smaller bill and, of course, a brownish head.

Female cowbirds are parasitic nesters that lay eggs in the nests of other birds. Sometimes the host species will immediately eject the cowbird egg; at other times, the host may abandon its nest entirely, or add a new nest layer of nesting material to cover or bury the cowbird egg. But often, the hosts become unwitting foster parents to a bulky, squawking cowbird chick with a hearty appetite. While the destiny of a given cowbird egg is uncertain, this parasitic lifestyle works well enough to ensure continuation of the species.

Cowbirds feed on insects, seeds, and grain gathered from the ground. As their name implies, they are frequently associated with herds of domestic cattle, taking advantage of insect prey stirred up by the roving livestock.

We have learned that fall wanderings of "accidental" species can be attributed to seasonal weather patterns or migratory misfires of inexperienced or immature birds. In the rare cowbird's instance, persistent southwesterly winds had gusted into New England for several days prior to his sighting. A second subtropical songbird, a gray kingbird, subsequently arrived at Ogunquit's Marginal Way a month later.

Déjà Vu

Here's a question for all sharp-eyed bird and feeder watchers out there: Are you repeatedly seeing the same birds each day at your feeders? Have those familiar chickadees, nuthatches, titmice, and woodpeckers that show up daily in your yard nested somewhere around the local neighborhood? The likely answer is yes. Occasionally, individual birds show distinguishing features, such as oddly-colored traces of plumage, or perhaps a missing or out-of-place feather or two. Unique behavior traits can also serve to identify your regular feeder customers. One particular blue jay mimics the high-pitched whistles of broad-winged hawks when approaching my feeders. Broad-wings nest nearby each year, affording the jay opportunities to learn and mimic their calls. The jay's vocal renditions convince some hawk-fearing songbirds to vacate the feeders before he lands.

From August through October, answering my leading question will get trickier, as troupes of far-flung migrants enter the local picture. By then, we'll see a mix of worn and faded, molting adults and fledgling juveniles with transitional physical resemblances to their parents.

This lively flow of migrants can trigger speculation over geographic origins and eventual destinations of some birds. In a few cases, however, a crystal ball is not required to resolve such mysteries. For several years, I've enjoyed sporadic contact with a leg-banded Canadian gull in Rockland. Banded as an adult at Ile Deslaurier near Montreal in April 2012, Gull BF2Z is a male ring-billed gull who, at the time of this writing, is at least eleven years old. He's a member in good standing at a forty-five thousand-pair nesting colony. By late summer, I anticipate his post-breeding returns to Rockland. This year's date was August 3, when I noticed a solitary, medium-sized gull atop the flagpole at Hannaford's parking lot. Driving closer, I focused my binoculars on the blue plastic band on his right leg: BF2Z was back indeed! Soon he sailed down to join me at ground level.

Several of my birding chums have experienced long-odds connections with sojourning birds, as well. My friend Mark once visited a fall hawk migration hotspot on Cape Sable Island, Nova Scotia. One day, an oddly-shaped raptor with tapered, pointed wings and a banded brown tail entered Mark's view. Was this a young peregrine or perhaps a northern harrier? No, the wing and body shape were all wrong for those. Instead, it was an immature Mississippi kite, a raptor of the southern United States that is relatively rare in Canada or even New England. Returning to Maine four days later, Mark resumed his raptor observations from the tip of the Harpswell peninsula. Mark's "best bird" that day was an immature Mississippi kite lazily drifting southward. The same bird? You be the judge.

More recently, my birding buddy Eddy had an ironic encounter in Biddeford with a vagrant species of hawk—an immature great black hawk. This extremely rare sighting represented only the second North American record for this Central/South American species. The first sighting had occurred at South Padre Island in Texas in May 2018. And, although Eddy was birding at South Padre that May morning, he missed knowing that the great black hawk was only a half-block away!

Now fast-forward to August 9, 2018. Following Eddy's move to Maine, he learned of the improbable great black hawk sighting in Biddeford. Eddy joined throngs of other birders from several states there to seek out the bird. Zing! The hawk perched cooperatively near a small pond and around various dooryards, as it patrolled for small birds and rodents. The odds of this mega-rarity travelling from Texas to Maine are extremely long indeed. But what about the much longer odds of Eddy and the vagrant hawk's eventual rendezvous in coastal Maine? Yes, detailed, comparative photos of the Maine and Texas hawks later confirmed it was the same individual.

Dovekie in the River

With limited time for extended birding sessions, I strive to take best advantage of discoveries during my routine daily travels. That means having accessible binoculars and a camera in my vehicle for particular moments when interesting bird situations may cross my path. I'm guessing that 90 percent of my bird columns involve local birds seen within a twenty-mile radius of my midcoast home.

A unique photo opportunity arose on November 13, 2015, as I crossed Warren's Main Street bridge. With legs jutting downward and open talons, two adult bald eagles skimmed low over the Georges River in attack mode. Eagles will stalk water birds by circling and hovering over them until their exhausted prey is eventually forced to resurface for air. Under this scenario, it was uncertain which party would fatigue first—the prey or the predator. For large, heavy predators like the eagle, sustained hovering motions rapidly deplete physical energy reserves. For the prey, it's a matter of remaining submerged and holding its breath, if it intends to survive.

Exiting my car, I stood on the river banking as the eagles continued their tandem efforts. After a couple of labored minutes, the pair abandoned the chase and perched in a lofted pine. Curious about their intended victim, though, I waited for the bird to resurface.

There it was! A small black-and-white duck, I surmised. Most likely a drake bufflehead. But gaining a second look, I saw that some features didn't add up to bufflehead. The head itself appeared rather small, and the black-and-white body patterns weren't quite right. And the bird's hunched, forward-leaning body posture didn't jive with my previous notions, either.

I studied the bird carefully through the magnifying lens of my camera. What an utter surprise. It was a sea-going dovekie this far upriver! At eight inches in length, the diminutive dovekie is the smallest member of the auk family in the North Atlantic (our Atlantic puffins are about 50 percent larger.) Dovekies nest in immense cliff-side colonies above the Arctic Circle and northwest portion of Greenland, centered farther north than other auks. Their Artic predators include glaucous gull, Artic fox, and even polar bears. The Inuit people also harvest the birds in springtime and preserve them as a winter food source.

Each fall, a portion of the dovekie population wanders southward. Pushed by fierce ocean storms and the pressing need for food, they generally appear in Maine's offshore waters by late October. Capable divers, dovekies forage for crustaceans and small fish just below the water surface, propelled by their wings and webbed feet.

These tiny auks have some strange history of popping up in unlikely places, as powerful ocean winds occasionally transport them miles inland. Such incidents are euphemistically called "wrecks." The more fortunate landing destinations are rivers or harbor environments. Since dovekies can't take off from land, grounded individuals face unfavorable outcomes. Winter blizzards result in birds being blown onto roadways and driveways. In the 1960s, an Aroostook County deer hunter found a dovekie in a mud puddle ten miles west of Ashland, Maine.

In days prior to my Warren sighting, a persistent nor'easter weather system had pummeled the coastlines, followed closely by strong southerly winds that may have deposited the auk into the upper river section. I watched the dovekie paddle its way downstream through flotillas of fallen oak leaves in the ebbing tide. One factor the hungry eagles couldn't have planned on: dovekies can hold their breath for several minutes at a time.

Fallouts

By one definition, a fallout of birds is "a mass of birds, exceptional in both number and diversity, that descends on a given locale as a result of meteorological or seasonal forces." Historical data indicates that fallouts are most likely to occur during the peaks of spring and fall migrations, and are usually associated with changing weather patterns produced by vigorous frontal systems. Taking off around dark, these nocturnal migrants transit southward throughout the night, to land the following morning for rest and sustenance. Finding themselves above open sea at pre-dawn, the weary night flocks descend to the nearest land formations. Being principally an eastern U.S. phenomenon, huge fall-outs are truly the dream stuff of birders.

My wife and I often spend a few pleasant days on Monhegan Island at the height of the mid-September bird migration. Monhegan can be a magical place to witness the migration. A well-known migrant trap, the island also attracts birders from all parts of the country. Under favorable conditions, bird-seekers are rewarded with exquisite views of neo-tropical migrants, raptors, and seabirds.

Over several decades, newly-arriving birders at the island's ferry dock have posed an accustomed question: "What's in Tom's yard?" This would be Tom Martin, a native of New York City, who has spent nearly fifty springs and falls at an upstairs fish house apartment midway along the island's main dirt roadway. Photographing and studying Monhegan's birds for decades, Tom catered a consistent May menu of fresh birdseed, spread out on scrap boards or pieces of plywood in his yard. This attracted scores of sparrows, migrant Baltimore and orchard orioles, and multi-colored rose-breasted grosbeaks. Tom also placed unshelled peanuts along his ramped entrance, and watched the blue jays carry them up island. Up until the early morning hours of September 25, 2009, the straight-forward answer to "What's in Tom's yard? was simple: "Not much." While a handful of warblers had foraged among the lilacs and apple trees lining the village roadways, southerly headwinds had stalled migration at places farther north.

Then an abrupt change of events came about. On the evening of September 24, a stiff northwest cold front whipped the island, rattling the house shutters and rocking the harbor boats. On the following chilled dawn, white caps bristled from the mainland. The brightening morning sky revealed hundreds of tiny, chipping birds, (or more likely two to three thousand), that landed and settled into cover across the island. Awed birders stood clustered at several roadside intersections as wood warblers, vireos, and thrushes infiltrated the trees and shrubs, in search of caterpillars and other insect fare.

Mesmerized, I stood with a seasoned birder as the zipping river of birds continued. A village cat had taken advantage of the situation as he scooted past us with a bird in mouth. As the feline and its feathered victim disappeared into thick cover, my birding companion exclaimed: "Hey!, that looks like a probable Kentucky warbler!" I was unprepared for what happened next. Shifting himself toward the thicket's edge, my companion dropped to his knees and began a noble effort to coax the cat back into view: MEE-OOW! The cat remained totally unimpressed.

As the fallout continued, flocks containing dozens of Baltimore orioles worked their way throughout the island. A few of the exhausted birds fed down in the dirt, in close proximity to the standing birders. The island lawns teamed with savannah sparrows and tail-bobbing palm warblers. Five different species of vireos were quickly observed. Over twenty species of warblers were tallied during that busy morning. And, finally, Tom Martin's yard contained the anticipated clay-colored, white-crowned and lark sparrows that managed to find him each fall. Tom was a happy man indeed. And we were happy too.

Lost and Found

As an inquisitive kid in New Harbor, I once made a ruinous mistake after discovering two baby robins that had separated themselves from a springtime nest within our neighborhood. The fledgling-sized pair was partially feathered and could flit a few feet at a hop. Failing to locate a parent robin or a vacated nest, a dumb but well-meaning impulse crossed my mind. I decided to "rescue" these unfortunate birds by taking them home. I fed them earthworms for a few days as they feebly followed me around our backyard. In the afternoons, (yes, eventually I took them indoors) they would roost contentedly amid my mother's crop of thick red hair as she watched television in our living room. One day, a neighbor suggested that we feed them some chopped-up bits of liver to "build up their blood and strength." The following morning, the spot-breasted duo lay dead and stiff and on the floor of their cardboard enclosure. So much for my trial-and-error rescue instincts. I had learned an important lesson, though.

Now let's swing to four decades later. It was October, as I trudged the perimeter of South Thomaston's Weskeag Marsh and spied a small shorebird standing quietly along an edge of pavement. I recognized this stripy little fellow as a juvenile semi-palmated sandpiper, which seemed somehow reluctant to fly. Each of my calculated advances was matched by the bird's equivalent retreats. Hoping to confirm his flightless condition, I rushed forward and captured the scuttling bird.

I held the one-ounce bird delicately in my hand to assess for injury. Physically, he looked fine. Despite his meager six-inch frame, I could sense his muscular vitality and strength as he shrugged his long wings to free himself. I knew this young bird had hatched somewhere in the northern tundra region and had completed, at a minimum, a several-hundred-mile, non-stop journey to Weskeag. His head was the size of my thumbnail, and his heart hammered mightily in my fingers. I was probably the first human figure this Artic recruit had ever encountered and, surely, the first person ever to touch him. "You are entirely waterproof," I informed him, admiringly. His mottled, tightly woven feathering served to withstand driving rains and cold winds. The smooth texture of his dark legs and feet felt like ultra-soft rubber boots. "You are exquisitely designed for what you do," I said.

The semi-palmated sandpiper is the most numerous of the small eastern shorebirds known as "peeps." Partial webbing between the outer toes (palmations) gives the bird its common name.

By mid-October, the majority of migrating shorebirds has already proceeded down the Maine coastline and arrived at wintering grounds between Florida's gulf region and northern South America. Most adults migrate south in late July to early August. Any shorebird found in October is most likely a juvenile making its initial southward passage. Migration is a perilous proposition for any bird, let alone an inexperienced juvenile on his first southern passage.

I sent the bird to the Avian Haven rehabilitation facility in Freedom, Maine. After careful examination, their director, Diane Winn, found no apparent injuries. The bird was reportedly eating well and would be flight tested in the facility's specialized cages in due time. If releasable, the young shorebird could be eventually transported to a release-point somewhere farther south. We must all wish him well.

Raptor Migration

Time spent gazing skyward in mid-September can be fruitful. On clear days, accompanied by brisk northwest weather fronts, legions of diurnal raptors move southward along lake fronts, coastlines, and hilled ridges. Chilled Canadian weather fronts, which provide assisting tailwinds, can spur pulsing movements of birds, with hundreds or even thousands of hawks passing an area in a single day.

I'm using the term "hawk" in a collective sense here, co-mingling the true hawks, such as the accipiters, with other diverging families of raptors.

During summer nesting, raptors are generally secretive, holding close to preferred nesting and hunting territories. Woodland-hunting sharp-shinned hawks prefer the tight cover of leafy forests, where they pursue prey in densely wooded habitats. By contrast, open-country falcons earn their living through swift and direct aerial pursuits. Sometimes these unique habitat clues can help to clarify a raptor's identity. You won't find a peregrine falcon nesting in a deep forest glen.

What raptors might we see during September and October migrations? For easterners, the possibilities include over a dozen species. There are three species of accipiters—goshawk, Cooper's hawk, and sharp-shinned hawk—three species of soaring buteos—broad-winged, red-shouldered, and red-tailed—three species of falcons—peregrine, merlin, and American kestrel. Northern harrier and osprey are the other likely possibilities.

Bald eagles of various age-classes silhouette the high banks of autumn skies. Later in the season, a few golden eagles pass along Maine coastlines from breeding grounds in northern Quebec. If we toss turkey vultures into the mix, there are ample opportunities to study and compare large fall migrants. Black vulture sightings are increasing in the Northeast, as these slightly smaller vultures expand their ranges northward. Other large, dark birds, such as northern ravens, are sometimes mistaken for raptors, especially when they soar among kettles of fall hawks high overhead.

It may seem counter-intuitive, but it is sometimes easier to identify raptors in flight. Decoding a distant, brownish lump perched on a tree limb or fencepost can be a challenging proposition for most of us. The "divide and conquer" strategy is a workable approach for hawk identification, though. Begin to narrow the odds by studying a bird's general shape, size, and, quite importantly, its particular manner of flight. Unlike those of brightly colored songbirds, raptors' muted feather tones may prove to be inconclusive. Distinctive patterns and markings, such as the red-tailed hawk's dark belly band, can be helpful and useful, however.

Here are some quick and basic differences between the various raptor groups: Accipiters are long-tailed, with short, rounded wings; they use a choppy "flap and glide" style of flight. Buteos are compact, chunky-bodied individuals with broader wings that are best suited for soaring on thermal air masses. Falcons have rather pointed wings, and their whipping flight style appears direct and purposeful. And with their lengthy tail and long-winged profile, harriers are lankier, with a distinctly buoyant manner of flight. And ospreys? Watch for their crooked, M-shaped wing profiles. When airborne, ospreys' wingtips tend to make them look "big-handed" rather than slim and pointed like gulls.

Although sky-riding hawks can be seen just about anywhere during migration, certain elevated sites with expansive views will increase your chances of spotting numbers of birds. In the midcoast region, these include Beech Hill in Rockport and Clarry Hill in Union. On some September days, raptors sail past the Maiden's Cliff summit at Camden Hills State Park, often at eye level. Along the Downeast coast, the summit of Cadillac Mountain at Acadia National Park has an active hawk-watch operation each fall. South of the midcoast, Bradbury Mountain in Pownal and Mt. Agamenticus in York should always be considered.

September Shorebirds

The span of fall bird migration occupies several weeks. And while migration is predictable in many ways, it is often an untidy process that offers up some unexpected bird sightings in its wake. The zenith of warbler and sparrow movements occur between mid-July and early September, as a mixture of adult and juvenile birds file south. Raptors, seabirds, and waterfowl will rule the skies in subsequent weeks.

For me, the members of the continent-hopping shorebird family are always worthy of study. Adult shorebirds begin their southward journeys in mid-July (adult females and failed nesters depart slightly ahead of the adult males). By early September, the fresh crop of crisply-marked, bright juveniles arrives from Arctic and tundra nesting grounds. These young individuals are often tame and confiding, and are readily viewed with binoculars or spotting scope. Here in Maine, it is possible to observe over thirty shorebird species throughout the migration periods.

Shorebird identification can seem a bit daunting, but, with patience and persistence, the task is achievable. Here are some practical considerations when sorting flocks of basically brown and gray shorebirds. Look at a bird's general shape and size. Is one larger or smaller than surrounding individuals? Feather patterning (dark and light areas) is often more important than subtle differences in actual color. How about the relative length of its bill and legs? What is its manner of feeding? Does the bird probe or dabble in shallow water or visually pick items from the surface? What is the surrounding habitat like? Does the bird choose to feed in open water or forage along grassy margins? Does the bird vocalize at all? Some flight calls, like the distinctive "tu-tu-tu" of the greater yellowlegs, are perhaps the easiest to remember. And finally, probability is a strong determining factor: What are the known odds of a species in question being present in your locality at that particular time of year? Check out the species' range maps in a reliable field guide.

Let's ponder three species that are superficially similar in appearance and general size. Each has a long bill and relatively longish yellow or green-toned legs. In each instance, their individual feeding behavior and specific bill shapes provide some clues leading to identity.

The greater yellowlegs is a common coastal fall migrant that breeds from southern Alaska to Newfoundland. As its name suggests, this active bird has vibrantly-yellow legs. The grayish upper plumage is strongly barred and speckled; the bill is straight with a slight upturn at the tip. This species employs darting, erratic, fish-chasing behavior in shallow marshy pools, but will also swim or wade up to its chest to cross deeper water.

The stilt sandpiper nests from upper coastal Alaska to James Bay, Canada. When feeding, it maintains a right-angle position with its head and neck, as it jabs methodically at the water surface. Due to its long legs, the stilt's feeding posture tilts forward, with tail pointing skyward. The bill is subtly downturned, or decurved.

Three races of short-billed dowitchers nest from southern Alaska to eastern Canada. The bill is rather thick at the base, and droops slightly at the tip. The bill of this "short-billed" species is actually quite long. The dowitcher's trademark behavior is its rapid, "sewing-machine-like" feeding style. In active feeding mode, dowitchers rarely lift their heads from the water. Being *tactile* or touch feeders, they nibble the water to retrieve food from the substrates.

For their ultimate survival, migrant shorebirds depend on food-rich staging sites such as Scarborough Marsh, Weskeag Marsh, and the extensive Thomaston Harbor mudflats. After fattening themselves for ten to fourteen days, these birds launch the next leg of their extended journey—the sixty-hour transoceanic flight to South America that awaits some species.

The Air They Breathe

For many types of birds, the months of August and September constitute the fall migration season. Migration occurs in graduated, short-hops for some, while others accomplish their lengthy journeys in a matter of a few days or weeks. What factors support such ready travel between regions and continents? Certainly, birds' lightweight skeletal structure, strongly developed flight muscles, and aerodynamic wing shapes are critical elements. But additional physiological factors are involved as well.

I'm thinking about avian circulatory and respiratory systems. By relative size, birds have larger hearts than all vertebrates, sometimes proportionately double in size to similarly-sized mammals. With each pump of the bird's highly-efficient heart muscles, the ventricles are almost fully emptied, whooshing oxygenated blood through all body systems.

For purposes of applied flight efficiency, birds' lungs are smaller, but more compact than mammals' lungs. They are much denser, however, and weigh as much as those of larger animals. Unlike mammals, birds do not have a straightforward, in-out breathing cycle. Instead, air passes in a somewhat continuous manner through a complex series of internal air sacs routing back to the lungs. Consequently, a nearly complete exchange of air volume results with each separate breath.

How do these physiological factors facilitate travel across vast distances? In general, powered-flight migrants have a wider availability of altitude ranges than do soaring birds that must rely on warm, thermal updrafts for lift. Much of bird migration occurs at altitudes of two to three thousand feet or higher. Endurance-flight specialists, like shorebirds, tend to favor the higher strata to gain advantages of reduced air resistance in the slightly thinner upper atmosphere.

Let's consider two diverse species that transit between Maine and the tropics each fall. Migrant flocks of semi-palmated sandpipers congregate at coastal marshes and mudflats in September. Mostly juvenile birds on their first southern passage, these six-inch sandpipers will spend a couple of weeks fattening up and adding to energy reserves required for the non-stop two thousand-mile ocean journey to northern South America. Depending on ambient weather and atmospheric conditions, this requires a sustained flight between forty to eighty hours.

Coastal flocks often begin their trek at peak high tides, since the flooded mudflats are then inaccessible to further feeding. After several gyrating passes to discern the compass bearing, the purposeful flocks proceed over the southeastern oceans. Prevailing westerly tailwinds aid their swift passage until they pass below the equator. Northeasterly wind flows then assert control, shepherding the flocks onto South American terrain.

Although shorebird migration is astounding enough, another small species, the blackpoll warbler, makes an equally arduous inter-continental jaunt. Migrant blackpolls accumulate between Nova Scotia and New Jersey coastlines in September, awaiting fall cold fronts that facilitate an express trip to the West Indies or South America. With a typical warbler flight speed of around twenty miles per hour, a migration of this length would typically require about one hundred hours—a physical impossibility for the warbler. With the addition of a thirty-mile-per-hour northwesterly tailwind, however, that same warbler would average a fifty-mile-per-hour ground speed to reach its destination within about forty hours.

The efficiency of avian flight easily outpaces energy expenditures made by mammals. It is estimated that a songbird flying a distance of one kilometer expends less than 1 percent of the energy that a mouse would use to run that same distance. For humans, relative energy expenditures are far higher. It looks like we'll all be taking the plane to South America.

The Larger Waders

Plaguing identification challenges associated with smallish gray and brown shorebirds in late August are somewhat alleviated when more sizeable and distinctive shorebirds arrive in Maine later in the season. When using the term "sizeable," I am referring to birds like the whimbrel and two species of godwits that stand about fifteen to eighteen inches tall. Given their notable sizes and shapes, these iconic shorebirds project a definite "wow" factor. Although other large shorebirds may be found in western regions of the country, whimbrels and godwits species are more likely to be encountered during New England's regional fall migrations.

Detailed scrutiny of their characteristic bill shapes will readily separate the whimbrel (long, dark, *downturned* bill) from the two godwits (lengthy, dark-tipped, pinkish bill with a slight upward sweep.) Hudsonian and marbled godwits are both seen along Maine coastline locations such as Scarborough area beachfronts and Weskeag Marsh's pools and low-tide mudflats. Migrating whimbrels are found across farm fields and open habitats, including the high blueberry barrens at Union's Clarry Hill, where they enjoy an assortment of berries, flowers, and insects. It is intriguing to watch these lanky birds feeding on waste blueberries as the bulge of swallowed berries proceeds down the whimbrel's long gullet.

Whimbrels and curlews are closely related. With breeding populations in North America, Europe, and Siberia, it is the most widespread of the curlews. The whimbrel's plumage is mottled grayish-brown and white, with alternating brown and white striping on the crown; the sturdy legs are bluish gray. Built for sustained flight, the powerful wings are long and pointed. It is no coincidence that the whimbrel's decurved bill conforms nicely to the burrow shape of fiddler crabs, a dietary staple in some parts of its range. Known as the "seven whistler," the whimbrel's call is a rapid fluty tu, tu, tu, tu vocalization, somewhat reminiscent of a yellowlegs.

Nesting on high arctic tundra, whimbrels and the godwits are paragons of long-distance migrants that routinely vault over entire continents. In May 2009, a female whimbrel, later named Hope, was fitted with a 9.5 gram solar-powered satellite transmitter on Virginia's Delmarva Peninsula. Then researchers tracked her amazing, nonstop flight to James Bay, Canada, where she spent several weeks before traveling on toward the Mackenzie River near Alaska. Eventually, Hope flew over to Hudson Bay, where she remained for the summer.

In September 2009, Hope began her fall migration trip. Leaving Hudson Bay, she flew southeast toward the Atlantic coastline. Crossing north of Maine, the bird continued her nonstop oceanic route and finally landed on the island of St. Croix in the U.S. Virgins Islands. Her exhausting flight had lasted one hundred hours and covered 3,550 miles. Although whimbrels generally winter in coastal South America, Hope chose to remain on St. Croix until April 2010. Then she returned to Virginia shores, pointing toward her tundra nesting grounds.

Tooty Fruity

There's a scientific term for birds that eat fruit—it's *frugivore*. During summer, insects provide the bulk of a protein-rich diet for growing nestlings. A number of species alter their diets to include more fruit, as the amount of available insect prey declines in fall.

Generally rich in water and carbohydrate content, fruit pulp provides excellent energy sources of sugar, playing an essential role in maintaining body heat in chilly temperatures. October's migrant robins, waxwings, blackbirds, and brown thrashers are drawn to coastal fruits and berries. Depending on the fruit's ripeness and the specific type of fruit, some birds eat the flesh, or sip the juice, or do both.

By virtue of their roaming travel habits, birds are effective dispersers of fruit seeds. Of necessity, the seeds must survive the bird's powerful digestive enzymes. Seeds pass rapidly through the digestive tract, becoming more water-permeable in the process. Consequently, this leads to higher seed germination rates.

I noticed a few rusty blackbirds huddled in apple trees on Monhegan Island, pecking at the ripened fruits there. Inhabitants of wet forested zones from Alaska to Newfoundland, rusties were also flipping decayed, water-soaked leaves in search of invertebrate prey. As their name implies, rusty blackbirds are tinged with rusted brown caps and backsides in the non-breeding period. Yellow eyes and a prominent, pale eyebrow are other distinguishing features.

Since the 1960s, 90 percent of rusty blackbird populations have quietly disappeared. In past decades, large single-species migratory flocks passed overhead. Presently, we must scan through mixed blackbird flocks to discern a few scattered rusties. If present trends continue, extinction of the species is possible in mere decades.

By October, another blackbird species, the Baltimore orioles, migrates. Lingering groups of young orioles resort to fruit as a convenient fall food source. On their neo-tropical wintering grounds, fruit constitutes a large portion of the oriole diet. That is why spring orioles so eagerly seek the halved oranges offered here in Maine.

Fall warbler diets? Warblers are considered as obligate consumers of summer insects. Consequently, most warbler species have withdrawn southward by October. And yet, limited numbers of hardy yellow-rumped warblers manage to overwinter along our beachfronts by feeding on fruits and berries. Yellow-rumps focus mainly on the fruits of bayberry bushes and the seeds of rugosa rose hips. Probing the foliage, warblers inevitably find bonus insect larvae hidden within the interiors of plants.

Planting fruit trees, berry shrubs, and other fruit-bearing plants is one productive way to feed birds on a budget. Such plants will help support vagrant flocks of winter waxwings and finches, such as pine grosbeaks. And by leaving some of the wind-fallen fruit on the ground, you will provide birds with welcomed food to sustain them through the leaner months of fall and winter.

Turkey Tales

The Thanksgiving holiday is an opportune time to consider turkeys. But I'm not talking about those thick-breasted, farm-raised birds, the ones that are pardoned and spared from the dinner table by the president of the United States each November. I'm talking about the wild turkey stocks, the primogenitors of all turkeyhood in Maine.

Back in 1970, Maine Fish & Wildlife began a successful reintroduction program, and today wild turkeys are an accustomed sight across much of the state. The wild turkey is the largest game bird in the United States, with five subspecies spread across the continent: Eastern, Osceola, Rio Grande, Merriam's, and Gould's. These sub-types vary in size, tail band color, and pattern, but Eastern birds comprise the largest segment of the population. Despite their considerable bulk, wild turkeys can run at speeds up to twenty-five miles per hour and fly at fifty-five miles per hour.

Wild turkeys are native to North America, with some historical and geographical twists along the way. The common turkey was tamed between 800 BC and 200 BC by the people of pre-Columbian Mexico. Up until about 1100 AD, the Pueblo peoples raised turkeys primarily for their feathers, which were used in rituals, ceremonies, and textiles.

Then, in the 1500s, European explorers carried wild turkeys back to Europe, where the birds were further domesticated. When early English settlers brought turkeys back to eastern North America a century later, the species crossed the oceans once again.

Part III: Moving into Fall

Today wild turkeys inhabit farmland, hardwood forests, and marshlands. Equipped with powerful legs and clawed toes, they are adept at raking through leaf litter and moderate snow depths. Their broad diet includes over six hundred types of fruits, nuts, waste grains, grasses, and insects. At night, wild turkeys roost in trees for shelter and protection from predators. Bearing in mind their large body size, the birds can easily fly into high forest perches.

Appearance-wise, the wild turkeys won't win a beauty contest. Males have blue or gray featherless necks and heads. When angry or during courtship displays, the neck and head turn a radiant red. The male toms are the larger sex, and boast a spikey "beard" of feathers protruding from the mid-chest.

The snood is a fleshy flap that hangs down from the beak; prominent bumps on the head and throat are termed as carbuncles, while the wattles drape from beneath the chin. These physical characteristics are far more pronounced in domestic strains of turkeys.

Most commercial turkey farmers breed birds with white feathers, because white feathers leave no spots on the skin when plucked. Bred exclusively for the table, flightless domestic turkeys are 70 percent white meat and 30 percent dark meat. These ratios differ from their wild counterparts, whose breast flesh is darker, deriving from their rigorous, muscular flight exercise.

Several falls ago, I witnessed a curious episode near Weskeag Marsh, when a sizeable tom turkey was struck by a speeding pickup truck on Buttermilk Lane. Hearing the dull thud, I witnessed an explosion of black feathers as the unimpeded truck roared onward. When I went to remove the carcass from the centerline, two gentlemen in an open-topped sports car careened over the rise. A large panting dog occupied much of the tight rear seat compartment. As they came to a skidding stop, the driver inquired directly: "Are you going to eat that thing?" "No," I replied. The two gents then opted to take the dog back home and return promptly to retrieve their roadside banquet. Bon appetite!

Wedding Doves

While attending a recent wedding at the rustic Beaver Lodge in Hope, I was reminded of our own wedding celebration there some years back. We had envisioned that the ceremony would culminate with an outdoor release of two white doves that would rise together ethereally into the heavens.

I had checked online and contacted the nearest vendor of wedding doves, a fellow located some ten miles away. That gentleman explained that, yes, he had some white homing doves, but they were young, inexperienced birds. "Wedding doves" are actually white pigeons that are selectively bred to achieve an appealing smaller size and sleeker profile. To train the birds, breeders must transport and release them at progressively longer distances from the loft, so the birds can learn their route back home.

Initially, the dove owner expressed mild misgivings about granting my rental request for his young doves, but my enthusiastic persistence won the day. On the morning of the wedding, I collected the two pristine doves and proceeded directly toward Beaver Lodge. Well, sort of. Somehow I made a few wrong turns and drove in a sporadic serpentine pattern of switchbacks for about a half hour.

Following our inside ceremony, the wedding assembly moved outside to witness the unified dove release. As anticipated, the matching birds spiraled gracefully skyward and completed a couple of sweeping circular passes above our heads. What happened next puzzled the onlookers, though. One dove returned to perch inquisitively on the lodge's chimney. Soon the second bird joined it.

I did my best to reassure our guests that the doves would eventually head safely back home, but matters quickly worsened. An adult goshawk streaked through the yard at eye level and glided like a heat-seeking missile into the wooded terrain beyond. Admittedly, the birder part of my brain thought, "Wow, a goshawk!" Fortunately, the hawk did not reappear, since the doves continued to loaf on the lodge roof for what seemed like hours. Eventually the dove pair vamoosed to parts unknown. I deemed it inadvisable to contact the dove owner to inquire whether his directionally-challenged birds arrived home.

Later on I pondered the whole experience. Were the young pigeons simply too inexperienced to find home? Or had their convoluted tour in my car confused and disoriented them permanently? According to avian researchers: "The 'map' issue, or a pigeon's ability to tell where it is in relation to where it wants to go, is different from the bird's compass system, which tells it which direction it's headed in." Two main theories suggest that pigeons either rely on their sense of smell to find their way home or that they follow the lines of the earth's magnetic field.

Infrasound is another important navigational aide. Because birds can detect low-frequency sound waves, well below the ranges audible to humans, they use sound to image the territory surrounding their loft area. This process is somewhat analogous to humans recognizing their home by sight. Particular areas of the world are confusing navigational zones, where birds repeatedly vanish or chose random compass headings contrary to their intended destinations. Other subtleties, such as local atmospheric conditions and peculiar terrain features, may also send birds in wrong directions.

So, if your future wedding plans involve an audacious live bird component, I would recommend handing your guests a bird-shaped, paper kite to fly and enjoy at their leisure at home.

PART IV

Our Coastal Winters

An Old Red Notebook

Combing through a box of written materials in preparation for a December Thomaston-Rockland Christmas Bird Count, I found a dog-eared red notebook brimming with historical data from previous bird counts. This simple notebook contained handwritten annual count tallies dating back to Rockland's initial Christmas Count in December 1970. I had acquired the notebook as a Mid-Coast Audubon board member back in 1994, agreeing to extend the chronicles of written log entries. When count data records became readily available on the CBC website, however, I ceased the notebook notations in 1998. But, owing to my continuous involvement with the Thomaston/Rockland Bird Count over several decades, this old red notebook is somewhat nostalgic to me.

A type-written letter by Porge Buck recounting background information about those early years was also enclosed. Porge and her husband, Lewis, were co-owners of the Craignair Inn at Clark Island in the early 1970s. She wrote: "Lewis coordinated the CBC in 1971. It was the first year that the count was recorded officially in *American Birds*, I think, although there had been counts that did not get recorded. He did all the correspondence and the center of the count circle was set (at 2.8 miles south of the Knox Mansion). The Mid-Coast CBC for 1971 was held on December 26: total species of 51; total individuals, 5697."

While much has changed since those times, central aspects of the annual bird counts remain constant. The founding concept of recording birds found within pre-determined fifteen-mile count circles between the dates of December 14 and January 5 remains unchanged. In 1900, Frank Chapman, an early officer of the Audubon Society, devised an annual "Christmas Bird Census," as an alternative measure to the traditional "side hunts" of those times. Side-hunts were competitive hunting events, usually held on Christmas Day, in which a segment of American hunters shot as much wild game as possible in a daylong hunting spree. Starting with a meager seventy-seven pioneering birders, comprising twenty-five count circles in 1900, the CBC now spans the U.S., Canada, the Caribbean islands, and Latin America. With over seventy-three thousand participants covering twenty-six hundred separate count circles, it is the longest running database of the natural world.

Obvious technological innovations have occurred since 1971. The calculative number-crunching powers of computers allow for in-depth, speedier analysis of data, highlighting bird population trends and the shifting distributions of particular species in response to our changing climate and habitat conditions. Continent-wide data indicate that numerous species are expanding their ranges northward or, at least, wintering farther north. Familiar species such as northern cardinal, mourning dove, and turkey vulture were uncommon in Maine's past decades. Red-bellied woodpeckers, of southern origins, are now found on a majority of Maine's thirty-one CBCs, and nest regularly in our state. Certain other species, like herring gulls, have declined due to localized habitat changes. Rockland's 1987 gull tally was 6,404, while present-day tallies have fallen to the several hundreds. What factors could have influenced the gull reductions? In 1987, Rockland's open dump site was in full operation and the local commercial fishing industry was prospering.

Since the early 1970s, birding optics have undergone remarkable advances that produce brighter, crisper images. Adding spotting scopes to the equation has heightened the odds of detailed bird discoveries. Today's birders also benefit from more comprehensive field guides that illustrate key diagnostic features of species and subspecies.

My customary Rockland CBC sector consists mainly of city neighborhoods, the transfer station, and portions of the waterfront. I'm certain to find scores of pigeons, starlings, and house sparrows. But occasionally, some unexpected wild treat registers on my personal radar, like that roving northern harrier that nearly struck my chest during a blinding, wet December snowstorm.

Are Birds Important?

Decades have passed, but a vivid winter memory lives in my recollection. I was scouting a wooded path in New Harbor and toting along my Daisy pump-style BB gun. Rounding a blind turn in the pathway, I came face to face with a great horned owl perched at about eye level on a horizontal branch twenty feet away. The bulky owl sat motionless, staring intently at me through its huge yellow eyes.

Several impulses scrambled my thoughts. I'd never stood so close to a formidable wild predator, especially one with such a well-storied reputation of flesh-eating plunder. The owl's fine, mottled feathering and prominent ear tufts were exquisite to behold. It was his densely-feathered feet and rugged, curved talons that drew my deeper attention, however.

Caught between spasms of wonder and fright, I weighed the options. Briefly I considered pointing the gun at the owl's chest to collect a possible trophy. A really bad idea, I reasoned. And what if the slightly-wounded predator lunged to attack me? Holding firmly to its perch, the owl sat unwavering as I gingerly retreated.

A second "trophy-taking" opportunity presented itself later that same winter as I skirted Mrs. Brackett's neighboring backyard. A group of starlings had clustered around the top of her warm, smoking chimney. As I contemplated the huddled mass, Mrs. Brackett opened her kitchen window and inquired of me: "You aren't trying to harm my birds, are you?"

"Oh no," I replied innocently, "I'm just watching them warm their little feet." Neither of us believed my explanation. This unsettling verbal interchange caused a temporary cessation in my Dennis the Menace lifestyle.

But let's face it. Surviving as a bird isn't that easy. Birds face hazards and obstacles everywhere, every single day. Consider the immense distances that neo-tropical songbirds must travel during migration, especially those nonstop crossings of the Straits of Florida and Gulf of Mexico. At its shortest transit routes, the Gulf waters alone measure five hundred miles.

Once they reach the U.S. mainland, hidden risks lie ahead. An estimated million migrants collide with towering lighted buildings and communication towers at night. In response, the National Audubon Society launched the Lights Out program over a decade ago, involving more than twenty major U.S. cities like Baltimore, Chicago, and San Francisco. In New York City, more than ninety buildings, including Rockefeller Center, the Chrysler Building, and the Time Warner Center now turn off bright outdoor lights between 11 p.m. and dawn during the peak spring and autumn migration periods.

Another one hundred million birds die in collisions with plate glass windows around our homes, when they grow confused by glass reflections that result in injuries and window-kills. Applying stickers or netting to windows can help a bit. Research suggests that placing bird feeders within three feet of the window (or affixed directly to the glass or window frame) is the safest distance. This lessens outcomes of high-speed window strikes. Alternately, feeders should be situated thirty feet or more away from windows.

One billion birds are killed by domestic and feral cats annually. We can't really blame the cats for their hard-wired hunting instincts. And, by the way, the fabled concept of "belling the cat" protocols have proved largely ineffective in reducing bird mortalities.

I hope you will savor every bird that finds its way into your yard and neighborhood. Each of them has worked so diligently to arrive there.

Caching For Winter

Of the several bird feeders in my yard, a hanging peanut feeder attracts steady lines of customers. Flitting parades of chickadees and fidgety bunches of titmice, nuthatches, and woodpeckers all take turns, maneuvering their bills between the caged metal mesh to retrieve fragments of nuts. The blue jays make concerted efforts to cull out whole peanuts through a frayed gap created a while back by gnawing gray squirrels. Since their wild diet includes acorns, beechnuts, and hazelnuts, the jays covet those fat-rich peanuts!

One jay in particular managed to cram a dozen peanuts into the gradually swelling crop in his throat. I figured he wouldn't eat them all onsite. Instead, like the chickadees and other smaller-sized nut harvesters, he would cache them for future use at dozens of secretive locations, with most being buried under grass, in ground leaves, or stashed behind loose tree bark at distances up to a mile away. Once food is hidden, birds may revisit the site periodically to adjust or rearrange the final placement, or perhaps to refresh their memories of the precise locations. Since some cached foods, like acorns, tend to shrivel in volume as they dry out, moving them around to new spaces makes practical sense. The seasonal time spans for gathering of food staples, such as acorns, spikes their intrinsic value as long-term assets.

How do birds remember all those caching locations? Species like chickadees and titmice temporarily increase their brain size in autumn. The hippocampus portion of the brain, responsible for long-term memory, grows in size in fall and winter and decreases once again in spring. It is hypothesized that other species with less long-term memory capacity may over-stock their territories with food and then re-forage the same sites throughout the winter.

Caching helps birds survive periods of bad weather and occasional food scarcities. Some species have favored menu items and cache sites. Chickadees prefer black-oil sunflower, often eating a small portion prior to caching the seeds under shingles, bark, dead leaves, or in knotholes and clusters of pine needles. Chickadees are more likely to cache during the midday. Titmice choose the largest sunflower seeds available to eat and cache, often stashing them within 130 feet of bird feeders. Nuthatches also prefer larger seeds, hiding them in deep furrows of tree trunks and the undersides of branches. Feeder studies indicate that birds show a 25 percent preference for shelled-out sunflower seeds.

In addition to supporting the well-being of birds, caching serves as a vital seed dispersal tool across forested regions. In the western U.S., for example, Clark's nutcrackers may store one hundred thousand white bark pine seeds a year.

Field observations suggest that the nutcracker's recollections of caching sites are maintained for seven-to nine-month intervals, long enough to span the hardships of winter. Since not all seeds are recovered, caching behavior creates some mutualized benefits in sustained nutrition for the birds and the subsequent renewal of forest trees.

Not all caching behavior involves plant materials, however. Ravens and crows routinely hide meat scraps. And a robin-sized predator of small birds and mammals, the northern shrike, temporarily warehouses its prey on thorns and barbed wire fencing. That way, the shrike can return later to finish its meal in leisure.

City Falcons

In certain winters, the city of Rockland hosts a pair of adult peregrine falcons that comb the city waterfronts in pursuit of rock pigeons. When the pair mounts the sky in tandem flight, the larger female member is easily distinguishable. Her smaller mate, the tiercel, may be slightly quicker and more agile of wing, but she is all about swift, physical power.

The falcons' schedule of morning raids follows a fairly predictable script. At night, most pigeons seek the warmth and security found beneath city wharves. On typical early mornings, lines of pigeons come and assemble on the utility wires and rooftops at the harbor's edge around 7 a.m. Other pigeons converge in the parking lots to gather grit, bathe, or take a sip of puddled rain water.

Once a streaking falcon enters the scene, two hundred pigeons erupt in chaotic unison. Their pigeon survival dance has begun, as panicked formations gyrate, tightening their ranks as best they can to reduce individual vulnerability. For best prospects of success, the falcon must cull out and isolate single pigeons from the swirling throng.

One recent morning, a falcon rocketed through the flock. It was the large female again. Swooping and diving, she initiated a full-on assault, her hard-whipping wings cutting the air with an impressive, audible whir.

Clearly, this was not a casual attack. In short order, she nudged part of the flock out over the open harbor, plunging vertically to snatch one fleeing member. Two herring gulls squealed at the falcon in shrill protest, and offered half-hearted aerial retorts. With sharp, lethal blows to the head, the falcon dispatched her victim and transferred it up harbor.

On this morning, the falcon dined atop the flat masthead of the windjammer J&E Riggin that lay at winter dockside. Flipping the stout corpse onto its back, she began tearing and removing layers of breast feathers. By some odd chance, a wafting, northerly breeze propelled the sinking procession of feather debris in my direction. One of the wispy body feathers tumbled and twisted lightly in the breeze. Drifting downward and ever closer, the severed feather landed, adhering exquisitely to the chest of my wool overcoat.

Coping with Winter

With October's dwindling daylight and dipping temperatures, many summer birds have retreated south for winter. These are species of warblers, flycatchers, and sundry songbirds that rely primarily on insects for sustenance. The daunting feat of migration itself, navigating stupendous distances and avoiding potential dangers, is a challenge that must be faced twice a year. For birds that nest during Maine's brief summers, but spend the majority of the year in tropical climes, it begs the question: Should we regard them as endemic Mainers or seasonal tourists?

Quantities of birds arrive or remain through Maine's winter months, however. This includes year-round residents, ranging in size from tiny golden-crowned kinglets to massive bald eagles. Several species of nomadic winter finches also visit occasionally, based on abundances of seed, cone, and berry crops farther north. Flocks of waterfowl relocate from the interior U.S. and Canada to winter on coastal bays and open-ocean. These over-wintering birds must manage two existential threats—freezing and starvation.

How do winter birds meet the challenges of staying warm? For starters, birds maintain a higher internal body temperature than humans—generally about 105 degrees Fahrenheit. Their primary strategies for preserving thermal resources take several means. Layers of insulating feathering are the most apparent physical barriers to cold. In extreme cold, birds fluff up their feathers, utilizing the trapped air for increased insulation. During overnights, chickadees and kinglets huddle within the relative protection of tree cavities. Studies indicate that night temperatures inside large, live trees are warmer than similar-sized holes found in dead trees. On frigid mornings, you might spot a chickadee or titmouse at your feeders, with tail feathers crumpled or bent from a tight, overnight tree cavity.

These tiny creatures also reduce core temperatures to conserve body heat as they enter a temporary state of torpor. Cold feet? The chickadees' feet probably stay cold most of the time in winter, but their feet don't actually freeze. Foot temperature is regulated at near the freezing point, so that the chickadee's inner body core temperature is not depleted.

Winter survival is essentially a matter of maximizing ingested calories while minimizing spent calories. "*Guilds*," or social groupings of small winter birds, may help to boost their survival odds to some degree. These roving woodland bands, often consisting of titmice, kinglets, nuthatches, and downy woodpeckers, are anchored by a few territorial chickadees. Multiple sets of eyes are useful in spotting food and predators, leading to improved health and safety.

How do water birds combat the numbing water temperatures? Once more, their tight, interlocking feathers play a key role. The feathers of geese are preened and oiled daily as maintenance against cold weather. While preening the individual feathers, geese use their bills to strip away dirt, debris, and water from feather surfaces. A quick shake or ruffling of feathers dries remaining moisture. How do loons, sea ducks, and gulls withstand ocean waters as winter "sea smoke" veils the horizons? The feet and legs of water birds have a counter-current heat exchange system. Veins and leg arteries are positioned close together, permitting warm blood flowing from the heart to heat up the colder blood returning to the central body. On land, these same birds have the added option of standing on one leg to reduce heat losses by one-third, or lying down to shroud their feet beneath layers of downy feathers.

Gallinule

One January afternoon, a Martinsville resident phoned about a strange bird in his side yard. "The bird looks like some kind of a heron," he said. "It is perhaps ten or twelve inches long, with long yellow legs and some bluish coloring on the breast." Suspecting that his mystery bird was possibly a gallinule, I went to investigate.

Upon my arrival in Martinsville, the green-backed wading bird stood midway up a snowdrift, rocking its upper body in a repetitive back-and-forward motion. This was indeed an immature purple gallinule! In a likely attempt to avoid frostbite, the bird stood alternately on its right and left feet. Understandably, this tropical bird seemed dazed and lethargic. The extremely long, slender toes, normally reserved for treading lily pads, were essentially nonfunctional and useless on the slippery, frozen surfaces.

Moving in closer, I rushed the bird and easily captured it by hand. With the exception of a slight right-wing droop, the gangly bird showed no obvious sign of injury. Once in my grasp, the bird emitted a protesting "kruk-kruk-kruk" vocalization that resembled a cross between a clucking chicken and a tiny trumpet.

I placed the bird in a cardboard box lined with an old bath towel and contacted Diane Winn at the Avian Haven Rehabilitation Center in Freedom. The bird was fully evaluated, given some hydrating fluid, and warmed up inside an incubator. While a typical adult gallinule weighs around 200 grams, the Martinsville bird's weight was only 139 grams.

Despite the best efforts of the experienced rehabilitation staff, factors related to starvation and possible disease resulted in the female gallinule's demise a few days later.

A member of the rail family, the purple gallinule is a chicken-like marsh bird sometimes called a "swamp hen." Adults are distinguished by their iridescent greenish back, deep purple-blue undersides, and stout reddish, yellow-tipped bill. The gallinule's normal range covers Florida and the Gulf states, the Caribbean, Central America, and northern South America. Oddly enough, this southern species makes periodic winter incursions into Maine and, occasionally, to Maritime Canada. There are a number of January gallinule records for Maine. With their rather awkward flight style and long, dangling legs, gallinules are considered to be rather weak fliers. They are able swimmers and have some climbing ability in low trees and thick marsh vegetation. Since it seems unlikely this tropical species would voluntarily abandon its warm southern climes in January, we might assume these wayward wanderers are swept up the northern coastline by surging winter storms.

Remarkably, Maine birder Reg Pelletier had discovered a "wrecked" gallinule on the nearby Rackcliff Island causeway in Spruce Head several years earlier, following a severe winter snowstorm. After being rehabilitated at Avian Haven, that bird was transferred to a Virginia wildlife center, to be enjoyed and admired by patrons of nature.

Inchworms

One recent Saturday, I went birding with friends at Pemaquid Point. Throughout my growing up in nearby New Harbor, I knew much of the point's rugged terrains on an intimate, inch-by-inch basis. Mere inches, coupled with elements of lucky timing, can play determinant roles in finding birds. Timing and circumstance can also result in permanent outcomes, where inches can impact our personal lives, as well.

In my late-teens, I could have easily perished at the Point. One winter morning, I slipped on a snow-covered ice sheet while traversing a high granite ridge north of the lighthouse. I'd toted along a shotgun, intending to ambush some surf-riding sea ducks. Without warning, I lost footing and fell, landing helplessly on my back. My prone body began a slow, terrifying descent down the rounded cliff face and toward the boulders sixty feet below. In one horrible instant, I recognized my probable fate. But then, my boot heels fetched on a two-inch line of crusted snow further downslope. It was just enough to interrupt my forward progress and imminent drop. Still fearing disaster, I rolled cautiously onto my stomach and inched up to safety—a treacherous, several-minute process.

Timing and circumstances matter. Not all threats of demise are as instantaneous or clear-cut as mine was on that fateful winter morning. Some threats inch their way along at a barely discernible pace. Human conservation-policy decisions influence natural outcomes in direct and irreversible ways. Over 190 species of birds have become extinct in the past five hundred years. Of approximately ten thousand worldwide species of birds, twelve hundred are presently ranked as being under threat, due to accelerating rates of extinction factors. Of one hundred and forty two native Hawaiian bird species, ninety-five has now vanished. Historical Canadian and New England extinctions include the great auk, a flightless, giant-sized member of the alcid family. The Labrador duck and the heath hen are others. A relative of the prairie chicken, heath hens were common in scrubby coastal barrens between southern New Hampshire and northern Virginia during Colonial times. These tasty birds were hunted extensively for food, as their numbers declined dramatically into the 1870s. A shrunken population of three hundred hens remained on Martha's Vineyard until around 1932, when the final survivors disappeared.

Undoubtedly, the most widely-publicized North American extinction is the passenger pigeon. In 1836, John James Audubon proclaimed the passenger pigeon as the most numerous bird species in North America, describing a mile-wide flock of migrating pigeons that passed overhead and blocked the sun for three straight days. By 1900, none survived in the wild. The last living pigeon, named Martha, was found dead on the floor of her cage at the Cincinnati Zoo on September 1, 1914. This most prolific of species had completely vanished within the span of a human lifetime.

Global rises in atmospheric and ocean temperatures are affecting the nesting outcomes of green sea turtle populations, as male turtle numbers are plummeting. The sex of sea turtles is determined by ambient sand temperatures of nest burrows during incubation. Warmer temperatures favor females; cooler temperatures produce more males. At roughly 85 degrees Fahrenheit, approximately equal numbers of each sex are hatched. One recent scientific study of about two hundred thousand turtles found that 99.1 percent of the juveniles were female and 86.8 percent of the sub-adults of the entire population were female. The mathematical implications here are inescapable.

Like the deliberate inchworm, humans are quite adept at measuring the status of our remaining wild creatures. Perhaps we should pause now and see how beautiful they are.

January Coots

At its fullest, watching birds transcends the straight-forward process of identifying a particular species through field observation. Further investigation leads to elements of deeper appreciation and understanding. For folks driving past Rockland's Chickawaukee Lake one recent fall and early winter, the spectacle of American coots feeding at lakeside drew rapt attention. Daily commuters on their way to work observed the mulling flocks. When the bitter cold eventually arrived, we all wondered how long this massive flock might remain at such a northerly location.

The lake had stayed remarkably ice-free for the December 17, 2011, Christmas Bird Count, when six hundred coots were tallied. Then, in early January, skim ice formed in the shallower parts of the lake. Seemingly unfazed, the flocks continued to dive for submerged aquatic vegetation in other sections of open lake.

One afternoon, an adult eagle attacked the flock as the birds sequestered in the water fifty yards from shore. The flock bristled in cohesive reaction, jamming together and forming an impenetrable, solid shield of dark bodies. Their frantic splashing motions probably added to the eagle's confusion and difficulties. After making a half-dozen unsuccessful passes, the tiring eagle abandoned the chase.

As January ice encroached, the coots made do by navigating through narrowing ice channels. By the morning of January 5, the lake developed a uniform sheet of skim ice, and the flock sat clustered in a thirty-foot circle near the shoreline. A few birds preened themselves, while others stretched their wings or legs. Some wandered for short distances, pecking at the ice surface. I watched them pick up and swallow a few shed body feathers and other tiny bits. Only a football field-sized patch of blue water was visible at mid-lake. Would they enter the lanes of open water today?

By late that afternoon, the flock was camped again by the highway banking for the night. Light, falling snow coated the lake, revealing the few wet, open slots. Early the next morning, I stopped to survey the scene. An irregular circle was etched into the ice surface, where the flock's collective body heat had melted a ring. The previous afternoon, a passer-by had tossed slices of bread out onto the ice. Now several gulls and a crow breakfasted on the frozen scraps. Two dead coots were frozen inside the mirrored ice surface, apparently trapped there during an attempted dive. The ruminating contingent paddled vigorously in the waters offshore! It was unclear whether their circular swimming maneuvers were intended to avert further ice formation, or meet some other social purpose.

By January 8, half the flock had vacated during the overnight, leaving behind about 220 birds in the final patch of open water. So what happened with Rockland's dawdling coot pack? Eventually, they were compelled to press southward or face freezing and starvation. That's how nature works. Neither cruel nor kind, it's just the way of wild creatures.

Just Ducky

Let's begin with a disclaimer: I don't pretend to understand exactly how ducks think or to know every motivation behind their actions. However, I certainly enjoy speculating from time to time, in human terms at least, about their compelling behaviors.

Numbers of wintering dabbling ducks congregate in mixed flocks amid sheltered waters close to food resources. Distinguished from the diving ducks, dabblers comprise those ducks that tip up to feed in shallow water. In the water, their bodies assume a higher profile than do divers, as they swim with tails held clear of the water. Dabblers are capable of vertical take-offs, rather than pattering the water surface. Most dabblers, such as mallards, American wigeons, northern shovelers, and teals are relatively colorful birds, with rectangular-shaped, iridescent speculum patches on the trailing edges of the wing.

Like other bird families, ducks alter their lifestyles throughout the year. For waterfowl, the fall-through-spring period serves as an extended session for mate-pairing, in preparation for spring nesting. Early courtship rituals become evident in winter, as ducks display exaggerated, head-bobbing motions to establish or strengthen pair bonds.

Some Rockport Harbor observations may be worth noting. Over a cup of morning coffee in my car one day, I scanned a flock of three hundred or so mallards near Andre Park. A drake wood duck swam casually amid the mulling throng of green-headed mallard drakes and their stripy, female companions. Wood ducks are unquestionably one of our most ornate and resplendent waterfowl. A common cavity-nesting species across Maine in summer, wintering wood ducks are infrequent visitors to the mid-coastal region.

At first, the wood duck's movements seemed random, but I soon concluded that his actions were focused primarily on a particular hen mallard. The drake shadowed her, as she maneuvered through tight zones of the flock. The drake proffered some bill-jerking motions to reveal the brilliant white feathering beneath his chin. Arching his neck, he flapped heroically and elevated his upper torso above the waterline, dramatizing his handsome rufous chest markings. At every opportunity, the drake positioned himself to emphasize his *good side* and the wagging mop of his impressive, shaggy crest.

Two mornings later, I returned to watch the duck huddle. Yes, the drake wood duck was still there. But things seemed different. Paddling aimlessly through the assembly, the drake appeared to be searching. He bypassed several unattended hen mallards, with no perceptible interest. Was this forlorn Romeo searching for his absent Juliet? Would no other lady duck suit his fancy?

Eventually the drake moved to a nearby shoreline, where a smallish hen mallard slept, her head tucked securely into her feathers. Approaching haltingly at first, the drake leaned forward with open bill and pulled her tail! He had roused her, and now she joined him in the water, where he lavished more attention on her.

Might this star-crossed couple have a future together? In strict biological terms, the odds of their sharing parenthood are low. They live in alternate universes. By his custom, he is an ordained cavity-nester, while she will occupy a ground-built nest in marshy terrain next spring. However, with more than four hundred hybridized combinations, ducks cross-breed more freely than any other family of birds. Hybrids usually acquire some intermediate physical traits from both parents, but the majority of waterfowl hybrids are reportedly infertile.

But, who knows? Mallards and wood ducks possess superior capabilities of hybridizing with a wide range of other duck species. In cases of mallard-black duck hybridizations, the dominant mallard genes are currently outpacing and, hence, replacing historical black duck populations across the Northeast. Christmas Bird Count data has documented this evolving trend for several decades.

Kids and Eagles

A December visit to a fifth-grade classroom at Thomaston Grammar School, where I'd gone to discuss eagles, triggered some childhood memories of my own. As a student at the Bristol Elementary School decades ago, I spotted an adult bald eagle wheeling high above the playground during a recess break. The eagle's gleaming white head and tail contrasted vividly with the dark blue sky. With over seven hundred eagle pairs currently nesting across Maine, you might think my Bristol eagle sighting was a routine matter. Well, that was not the case. The 1960s was an era where extensive use of DDT pesticides had decimated osprey and eagle populations, leaving Maine with twenty-one eagle pairs. Rachael Carson's evocative 1962 book, *Silent Spring*, sounded the environmental alarm, and DDT was banned from use in the U.S. in 1970. In following decades, Maine eagle numbers slowly rebounded under the watchful eye of Maine Fish & Wildlife biologists and state game wardens.

Upon entering teacher Lynn Snow's classroom, a live Florida webcam, featuring an active eagle's nest, was projecting from a laptop onto a wall screen. The eagle mates, Romeo and Juliet, were incubating their clutch of eggs. Lynn's eager, observant students already understood quite a lot about this pair. To avoid intense summer heat conditions, southern eagle populations nest during the cooler winter months. Once the Florida nestlings fledge in April, a few individuals may eventually trace the Atlantic coastline and wander north into Maine and beyond. By mid-March, our own Maine eagles will launch their breeding season by upgrading their existing nests.

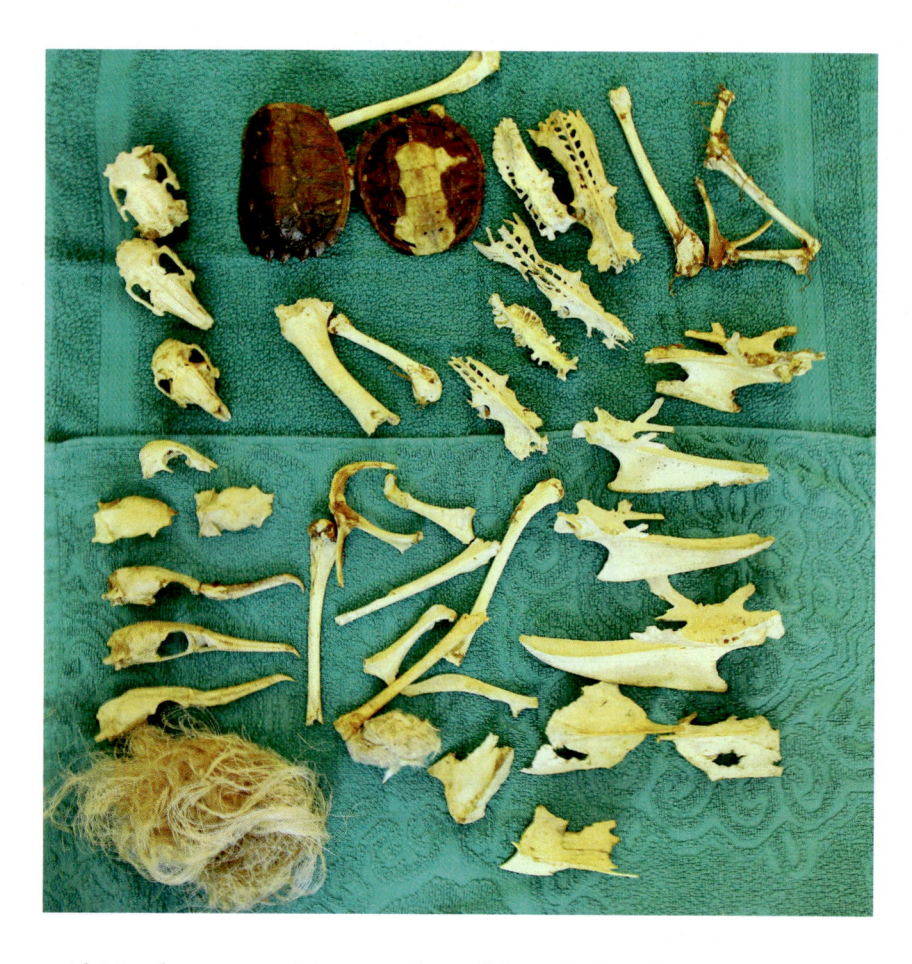

    I'd brought along a collection of eagle artifacts to the Thomaston classroom, some natural items recovered from the ground, where a perennial Warren nest had collapsed after a winter storm some years back. My pine-draped basket of green sprigs held an assortment of skeletal bird, mammal, and turtle remains that represent the typical eagle's fare. The diet of Maine eagles differs somewhat, depending on their regional locations and available food resources: The eagles' inland and northern dietary content is approximately three-quarters fish, while coastal diets are roughly three-quarters birds and one quarter fish. At the coast, sundry gulls, ducks, and summering cormorants are found in higher abundance than in inland areas. Slow-reacting double-crested cormorants become relatively easy targets, as they must taxi on water for take-off. Being relentless opportunists, eagles will grab a meal wherever and whenever possible.

Several students eyed my basket, where its mystery contents remained concealed by a hand towel. Did the basket contain an eagle skull, one asked? Was the greenery in the basket from a real eagle's nest? Would the kids be permitted to touch the items? One student asserted, "I am a very curious person!"

"Me too," I said.

"Yuh, I also check my house for hidden Christmas presents," she giggled.

"Me too," I answered.

Soon we placed the shrouded basket on the carpeted floor as the kids nestled around it.

The kids carefully surveyed breastbones of several bird species, each with its characteristic profile of a boat keel. Some keels showed puncture marks from the eagle's powerful bill. Cormorant skulls, with their hook-like upper mandibles intact. Feather-weight bones, with latticed skeletal frameworks. Skulls of three small mammals, whose fates were likely sealed when they attempted to navigate the open river. And carapaces of young snapping turtles, possibly snatched from their sunning rocks.

The pine basket also contained a shiny fishing lure and a fist-sized clump of abandoned monofilament line of some riverside fisherman. Kids were quick to recognize the potential dangers of such items around eagle nests, recounting experiences when they had retrieved similar debris from ponds and lakesides. With luck, they will become our environmental leaders and future keepers of eagles and much more.

NIMBYs

Most of us are probably familiar with the acronym NIMBY, which stands for "Not In My Backyard." For humans, opposition to potentially controversial projects near to home, like proposals for hazardous waste facilities, power plants, and landfills or electrical corridors may elicit NIMBY responses. The possible list of issues leading to such opposition is linked to our individual perspectives and life priorities.

But NIMBY situations aren't restricted to our human endeavors. Birds react negatively in certain situations they find threatening. For birds, NIMBY-qualifying events fall into a couple of broad categories: life-threatening incursions by predators and seasonal competitions for high-value nesting territories. One week, I witnessed examples of both scenarios, less than a quarter mile from my Warren driveway.

On successive days, a noisy murder of crows assembled around a small patch of woods behind my house. Crows are animated, active creatures, highly vocal through the daytime hours. Their darting swoops and dives seemed to pinpoint a towering white pine tree poised among a copse of shorter maples. The deafening cacophony meant just one thing: a predator was lurking somewhere close-by! I'd made previous, unproductive ventures into the wooded glen to analyze the scene. Each time, the crows would suspend their raucous mobbing, and temporarily disband, despite my best efforts to make a stealthy approach.

During a subsequent bout of mobbing, I entered the woods with camera in hand, committed to hanging out for a spell to learn the root cause of these disturbances. As the crows retreated in silence once more, a lone blue jay added a throaty note of protest from overhead.

Peering up to scan the bare pine limbs, I saw nothing. Then, I sensed a presence, a set of dark-brown eyes, framed through a tight portal of branches and leaves. A barred owl leaned forward to survey me cautiously. The hunkered owl was fully shielded from direct crow strikes by a thick web of branches. In actuality, a great horned owl is probably a more legitimate threat to night-roosting crows than a rodent-eating barred owl. In crow-think, any predator is still a legitimate and potential enemy, however.

On a different January morning, I heard high-pitched, chittering calls coming from the riverfront below my house. Two pairs of adult bald eagles were engrossed in discussions over an apparent territorial issue. Since nesting activity wouldn't commence until March, what was the big concern that created so much ruckus? Once a permanent nest site is established, eagle pairs occupy and defend the territory around the immediate vicinity throughout the year. In extreme northern interior sectors, where river systems freeze up in winter, eagles may stray southward from Canada and elsewhere. Those particular pairs must return north well before spring to regain possession of their territories.

Given the current time of year, it was possible that the Warren intruders were visitors from somewhere inside the state. Maine's eagle nesting population now exceeds seven hundred pairs, so future competitions for quality nesting locations are likely to increase.

Separated by 150 yards, the two sets of eagles sat anchored in riverside trees in a staring, screaming showdown of wills. No physical contact was needed to settle the matter, as the two visiting birds eventually made a back-door exit upriver. The bragging rights of ownership accrued to the steadfast local nesters.

Owl Moon

Well, I did it again—spent another night of sleepless travel on the byways of Somerville and Palermo, Maine. This was my accustomed owl-monitoring circuit. For a decade, I'd volunteered for the Maine Owl Monitoring Program. This statewide study was focused on several common species of nesting owls, hoping to learn more about their populations and distribution across Maine. Primarily, the study involved the northern saw-whet, barred owl, great horned owl, and the less common long-eared owl. Scattered eastern screech owls also turned up randomly on a couple of survey routes.

My fifteen-mile route included a variety of habitats, with each of the ten pre-determined roadside stops located at least one mile apart. After an initial period of passive listening, a series of three successive recordings was played to elicit owl responses. The first recordings involved the smaller species; subsequent recordings moved on to progressively larger owls. Compared with some coastal routes I'd tried, this inland section was far richer in owl numbers. The surveys began at midnight, and lasted about four hours.

At Stop #1, a rising orange moon shown through the silhouetted tree line. I got off to a decent start here—one great horned owl (GHOW) hooted from a considerable distance off. At Stop #2, a vocal group of geese honked repeatedly from a nearby pond, masking potential owl calls at times. During the final minute of that listening session, a single barred owl spoke up. From experience, we knew that barred owls often wait several minutes before eventually responding.

Aside from the personal challenge and motivation of finding a bunch of owls, it can be downright boring when you visit several stops with no results. And, when you stand in freezing temperatures for extended periods, your mind begins to wander and your initial enthusiasm wanes just a bit…"I must be nuts standing out here in the cold!"…"Humans weren't meant to inhabit lonely, dark places alone"…"Oh, great, here comes that rattling car with the dragging muffler again." Meanwhile I note the high-cruising jetliners heading silently east for Europe. I marvel at the blaze of a streaking shooting star.

Stop #5 produced a second hooting barred owl. When I exited the vehicle at Stop #7, a diminutive northern saw-whet owl tooted his staccato liquid calls from a back field in the near distance. Sounding like a miniature version of a backup beeper on heavy equipment, the owl persisted forcefully for several minutes. When I eventually played the saw-whet tape, he fell temporarily silent before resuming his tooting in earnest. As I subsequently played the barred owl and great horned owl recordings, the little saw-whet continued to hoot, unfazed by the larger voices. Contrary to our common logic, this small owl willfully betrayed his presence with potential predators hooting close-by.

At Stop #8, things really picked up. Two barred owls! From one hundred feet away, one owl uttered his sharp "Who-cooks-for-you?" vocalizations. Its mate answered somewhere in the background. During the first two playback sequences, the birds had remained silent, but, after I aired the great horned owl call, they went ballistic! Next, the pair moved in unison to the roadside, where they engaged in a shrill duet that progressively gained in volume and intensity. Their eerie cacophony sounded like two unruly monkeys contesting a banana. The nest was undoubtedly somewhere in close proximity.

On my final stop, a male woodcock twittered and cheeped overhead, doing his springtime sky-dance ritual for a prospective mate. The timberdoodle landed within a few feet of me and delivered his dry, nasal "peent, peent" courtship notes. Suddenly, a deep-throated barred owl uttered a wavering, eerie "woooooo," a quarter mile down the road.

It had been a successful night: five barred, one great horned, and a single saw-whet owl. I'd felt privileged to share the night woods with these feathered insomniacs. On the other hand, I also felt grateful that I'd be sleeping soundly throughout the following night.

Raven on a Mission

It is eleven degrees Fahrenheit outside and snowing lightly, when I step into my backyard. Posing in a state of calm watchfulness, a huge raven occupies a tall, weathered stub two hundred feet away. This is his sentry post. For three weeks, the solitary raven had held vigil over a partially snow-covered turkey carcass I had tethered outside. Recently, I'd even added a few beef neck-bones and chicken hearts, to supplement the meaty cache.

A daily circus of scavengers, including three red-tailed hawks, assorted crows, and several roaming herring gulls, competed for these precious winter rations. Notably, it was the raven that served as the ringmaster of this revolving menagerie.

When an adult bald eagle abandoned the premises for bigger treasures, the raven assumed dominance over the remnant bones and meat scraps. His native intelligence, muscle power, and guile showed that he was well up to the task.

One afternoon, an adult red-tailed hawk, a small-framed male, I would estimate, arrived to inspect the cache. Once the hawk descended to feed, the vigilant raven intervened decisively, landing within two feet of the grounded raptor, raising and spreading his four-foot wings to their widest dimensions. Opening his gaping dagger of a bill and puffing up his feathers, the raven pressed forward. His slow, mechanical wing-waving motions forced the dumbfounded hawk backward onto his haunches.

For the record, red-tailed hawks are not physical slouches by any means. They are formidable predators, with powerful, sharp talons. In this case, the male red-tail appeared to be way overmatched. After an ineffectual wing-spreading reprisal of his own, the defeated hawk withdrew. The following day, the red-tail received worse treatment, as the raven pecked at his face and knocked him over.

In the next hawk interaction, a robust female red-tail fared only slightly better. Closer to raven-sized herself, this was an immature bird with a grayish, dark-banded tail. It takes successive years of feather molts to acquire the adult's trademark brick-red tail. For the most part, she stood her ground and scrapped in earnest with the raven, but eventually vacated the scene.

A day later, the small male hawk returned, this time with a sizable adult mate. Together they presented a more unified front against the raven's hostility and were able to secure some scraps. Once more, body size was an operative factor, as the larger female claimed a majority share.

Hardy denizens of northern regions, ravens are well adapted to rugged winter climates. Following a recent snowfall, my yard raven scooped away several inches of snow with his broad bill to unearth the subnivean cache. Raven pairs are often seen patrolling highway sections in search of road-killed animals. Besides their superior size, ravens are distinguishable from their crow cousins by a large, bulky head and heavy bill structure. Their longer-winged, fluid flight style and wedged-shaped tail cinch the identification.

The best surprise came one afternoon as the crafty raven fed alone. After gazing skyward for a minute or so, he purposefully lay down in the loose snow, stretching out and flattening his body contours. What was this odd behavior all about? My answer came quickly, as three herring gulls dropped from the sky and landed near him. By lowering his body to conceal the bones, the raven successfully hid his cache from the gulls' view. And they tell us birds are dumb.

Stakeouts

Stakeout: (stɑk'out) noun. "Surveillance of an area, building, or persons, often by police." Birders are also known to indulge in this practice whenever rare or unusual species are reported.

I'm not really a bird chaser, willing to travel long distances to see a particular bird, but I've participated in a few stakeout sessions through the years.

In the winter of 1975, an adult Ross's Gull was found in the Newburyport/Gloucester, Massachusetts area. It was the first sighting of this dainty, pink-breasted gull species anywhere south of Alaska. Understandably, its presence attracted droves of birders from all corners of the U.S. and beyond. Then-Secretary of Defense James Schlesinger (a competent birder who had obviously traveled broadly) reportedly jumped from his car to spot the bird, accompanied by a security detail. It was Roger Tory Peterson's 668th bird for the U.S. and Canada. Photos of the gull made the front page of the New York Times and were featured on national television networks. Dubbed as the "bird of the century," this single sighting was a probable catalyst for bird-watching enthusiasm in the U.S.

When a Boston birding friend invited me for a weekend excursion to Gloucester, I packed up and went. Exiting our vehicle on Gloucester's Eastern Point Road, I was unprepared for the pandemonium there. Cars lined the length of the narrow streets, and uniformed police were directing and diverting traffic!

The Ross' had been seen on the previous day at nearby Niles Pond, an ice-rimmed pond of several acres. As our party approached the pond's perimeter, I began to absorb the full context of the situation. Legions of birders equipped with spotting scopes and immense cameras on tripods enveloped the circumference of the pond. Scores of gulls of several species drifted lazily overhead, some landing to swim and bathe in the open water. With the arrival of each new gull, one hundred pairs of binoculars pivoted skyward. Glaucous and Iceland gulls (check); ring-billed and herring (check). A few great-black-backed gulls completed the list of typical wintering gulls. Alas, the Ross' never appeared that day. Satisfied with an exciting field experience, (drake king eider and harlequin ducks from the breakwater), I returned to Maine.

My recent winter stakeout situation was much closer to home—a female painted bunting that had lingered in a Rockland neighborhood for a spell. Painted buntings are colorful southern birds that wander north at times. The male's patchwork hues of bright blue, green, and red plumage are remarkable to behold. Rockland's female bunting was a more-or-less nondescript greenish-backed individual, with a faint eye-ring.

The accommodating Rockland homeowner said that the bunting favored a certain back-yard feeder in early mornings. The bird had reportedly suffered a recent leg injury. Pointing down at her own tiny ankle, her young daughter explained: "The bunting has a boo-boo." I also met the family's friendly black Labrador retriever, who liked me a lot from the start.

Stationing myself behind an eight-foot ornamental cedar tree, some sixty feet from the feeder, I prepared for a long haul. Optimism reigns high at the beginning of stakeouts. After a half-hour stint though, I headed off to work.

Early next morning was extremely cold. As I settled behind the cedar tree, the family dog appeared in the fenced yard area. He didn't notice me. Eventually he wandered toward my position and sniffed suspiciously. The dog advanced to within six feet, with just the spindly tree and a picket fence separating us. I did my best impression of a statue. Would he discover me and blow my cover? Now the Lab stood stiff-legged with his necked craned in a "cocked and loaded" posture. My scent was definitely carrying his way.

Suddenly, the dog barked with a sharp, exclamatory yelp! His bark seemed to startle us both equally. I stepped forward and patted his head. The dog wiggled himself and wagged his tail feverishly. He remembered me!

Let's just say that my stakeout strategies are a work in progress.

A 2014 Snow Job

With our winter bonanza of snowy owls in the Northeast, owl encounters are a pleasant reality for coastal birders these days. To illustrate, by early winter in 2014, I'd recorded six separate snowy owls within a ten-mile radius of Rockland.

One errant owl was discovered in an abandoned Portland office building on January 15. Possibly attracted there by resident pigeons and rodents inside the building, the owl was later rescued by a falconer and taken to the Avian Haven Wild Bird Rehabilitation Center in Freedom.

The owl, an immature female, was reportedly in good physical condition. After receiving a nourishing diet of chopped mice for several days, the owl was released off West Meadow Road in Rockland on January 18. Since many snowy owls tend to venture toward the coastlines, a coastal release site was preferred.

My wife, grandson, and I were fortunate to witness the bird's liberation as two Avian Haven volunteers unloaded a large cardboard carrier box. When the box lid opened, the owl sprang forth and launched herself gracefully over the grass tops, pumping her way down the field edge. Then she gained altitude and perched briefly atop a skyline utility pole to survey the new scene.

Unprecedented owl sightings in 2014 provided valuable opportunities to increase our firsthand knowledge of the species' life habits and hunting practices. One particular snowy had captured ducks at Biddeford Pool to supplement its standard rodent fare. Well equipped for long-distance travel, snowy owls navigate vast stretches of tundra in search of food stocks to support nesting activity. In years of food scarcity, the females may totally abstain from egg-laying. Along the coastal fringes of their breeding grounds, these powerful predators are known to head offshore to hunt dovekies, a tiny black-and-white cousin of the Atlantic puffin. Here in Maine, it should be no surprise that these rugged owls are drawn to coastal islands, where the potential for waterfowl and rodents is high.

Determining the precise age and sex of snowy owls can be somewhat complicated. Adult males are generally whitest, but there is a broad continuum of spotted and barred plumages that are linked to the specific age and sex of individual birds.

Once again, birders and photographers can make useful contributions. Project SNOWstorm, a collaborative research project, solicits flight photos of snowy owls. To quote the project's website: "In first-year owls, females have more bars than spots on the middle secondaries, where males have more spots than bars. Young snowies with four or more bars on the tail are generally female, while those with two or fewer are males."

Like all raptors, snowy owls ingest sizeable chunks of meat and whole smaller animals, such as mice. The indigestible parts, such as bones, claws, and fur, are formed into pellets that are regurgitated periodically to make way for subsequent meals.

PART V

For Birders' Eyes Only

Birds and Kids

It's been said that our current generation of children is the first one that chooses not to go outside. There are possible reasons for this phenomenon, including the growing fascination with hands-on technologies that offer games and other indoor indulgences such as messaging, texting, tweeting, and experiences in virtual reality. I don't intend to disparage these technological trends, but wish to encourage adults and children alike to venture outdoor. There are definitely lots of things to see and learn there.

Through sharing of natural experiences, my grandchildren's interest and knowledge of wildlife flourished. It began with watching chickadees coming to snatch sunflower seeds from my bird feeders. My front yard holds several seed and suet feeders that attract morning processions of birds. Next to my living room picture window is a laminated poster card, depicting the common songbirds of eastern North America. An old pair of 7x35 Nikons rests on the window sill, just in case they're needed.

Early in life, my granddaughter Haili began learning songbirds, and how to distinguish between "girl" and "boy" woodpeckers by checking for the red patch (or lack thereof) on their napes. As a four-year-old, Haili attended a sizeable social gathering with her mom, with mostly adults in attendance. When a small gray, crested bird landed on the porch railing, the puzzled adults pondered its identity. When Haili announced that it was a tufted titmouse, the adults graciously ignored her opinion. A day later, some of them were surprised to learn that she was indeed correct!

My grandson, Adrian, followed a similar path to nature. As an infant, he showed obvious interest in tracking the movements of birds and squirrels around my neighborhood. At about one-year of age, he began to emulate my "pishing" sounds as we searched out birds in the backyard. Pishing, (a.k.a. "spishing") is nothing more than producing a repetitious series of "pish, pish, pish" sounds, sort of like shushing someone to be quiet. The reasons behind the efficacy of pishing remain unexplained. Perhaps the rhythmic, scolding sounds mimic the alarm calls of chickadees and titmice. A variety of squeaking notes and kiss sounds (made by kissing the back of your hand) are often added for variety and increased effectiveness. The wavering, whistled calls of eastern screech owls produces similar attractant effects on songbirds, enticing mixed-species flocks to come forth and to mob an unseen predator.

During one June morning stroll, our combined pishing methods were richly rewarded, as a couple dozen birds jumped into plain view along a wooded edge. A contingent of chickadees, nuthatches, kinglets, a downy woodpecker, and several warblers flitted within inches of our faces. As I pished, Adrian stared intently at my lips for several seconds. Then he began his own round of pishing. Now, when Adrian visits, he heads toward that big picture window to check if the feeders are full and grab the binoculars. I guess it remains a toss-up which of us has more fun.

Birds of a Different Feather

In writing a bi-weekly bird column over the years, I have strived to highlight local birds of potential interest to readers. By their very nature, birds are creatures of grace and beauty that add a dimension of wonder and natural inquiry to our lives. Sometimes, for reasons outside their control, birds aren't always so appealing to the eye. Just as people experience illnesses or physical misfortunes in life, so too do wild birds. Recently I encountered two such examples of Rockland birds struggling with feather issues in different ways.

I noticed an American crow with warty growths on parts of its head and body. This crow had a viral infection called avian pox that can result from bites to bare skin areas of the body from mosquitoes, mites, fleas, and flies. The virus cannot penetrate intact skin, but can follow pathways through skin wounds or the soft tissue areas around the face, eyes, legs, or feet. Similar to chickenpox in humans, this virus runs its course, but may result in the eventual death of an infected bird, if its eyes or breathing apparatus becomes compromised. Birds that survive the virus develop immunity to future outbreaks. Diane Winn, director of Avian Haven Rehabilitation Center in Freedom, Maine, explains that infected birds can be successfully treated and released in some cases. She had recently treated a fledgling northern mockingbird at the Center that was later released. This bird-specific virus can't be transmitted to humans, but can spread to other birds through sharing common or communal sites, such as feeding stations or watering areas.

An adult great black-backed gull that had fouled its feathers in some type of red sludgy substance was the second bird in turmoil. Its underparts were thickly coated from the upper belly area to the end of the tail. To its best ability, this large gull was busily cleaning itself with comblike bill movements. Although the bird was a genuine mess at the time, the wings were free of debris. Oil or other exterior contaminants stress a bird's entire body system. On the other hand, healthy feathering keeps birds warm and dry by preventing air and water from penetrating to the body skin surfaces. After a series of oil spills in past decades, scrupulous techniques were devised for cleansing oil-soaked birds and animals using detergents, followed by judicious rinsing and drying procedures.

In the case of the Rockland gull, the bird survived his unsightly ordeal and removed most of the patina of reddish residue over a period of several weeks. Given a fighting chance, birds are true survivors.

Caps and Such

What basic gear does one need to watch birds? Well, a good bird field guide (I like the *National Geographic Guide*) and a set of binoculars are starters. A spotting scope is a convenient tool for getting detailed looks at distant birds, but is not a true necessity. You don't really need highly specialized clothing, but a hat or cap is often advisable for protection from the elements. Hats and caps reduce sun glare on the eyes, give some protection from harmful UV rays, and keep heads warm and dry in winter and shaded in summer. Certain hats can even reveal telltale characteristics of the wearer. Through the years I've gained a collection of birding caps that have benefited me in the field. A few caps were gifts from generous birding friends. And one hat in particular satisfied my sense of personal expression and whimsy, as well.

The other day I pulled a cluster of caps from my top closet shelf. Some models looked fresh and almost new, while the sweat-stained rims and visors of others portrayed their history of multiple days afield. Each of the hats bore some form of logo design, commemorating a birding festival, a birding hotspot, an environmental organization, or an individual bird species of note, such as a Connecticut warbler. That warbler cap has a double appeal to me as a reminder of spring excursions to the Connecticut Ornithological Association's annual meetings. In addition, the cap is a temporary substitute for the actual living bird itself. Despite years of birding, I've yet to encounter a Connecticut warbler in the flesh. Maybe next fall on Monhegan Island…

And speaking of Monhegan, I own a couple of island-themed caps from my favorite Maine birding destination: One cap reads "04852," the island's zip code. The other island cap features the iconic head of a goat, symbolic of the nimble-footed goats that graze the knobby slopes of adjacent Manana Island.

I'll share a few other caps with you. As a field-trip leader during the 2006 American Birding Association National Convention in Bangor, I wore a blue Maine Audubon leader's cap. A greenish cap from Cape May, New Jersey, holds fond memories of that renowned birding mecca. I've watched kettles of hawks soaring above the Cape May Point hawk watch platform, a fall raptor hotspot, before they commenced their cross-bay venture. By day, small groups of reclusive long-eared owls also skulked in nearby dense wooded sections. To my amazement on one twilight evening, seven of these majestic owls emerged to circle the Cape May Lighthouse tower like giant, slow-motion moths.

Following my surgical aortic heart valve replacement in 2016, I commissioned a dozen caps bearing a customized logo design. I had come to realize that several of my birding companions shared a similar medical outcome:—with each of our surgical successes, a bovine replacement valve had been installed. We jokingly made cow references, like our special yearnings for ice cream at Dairy Queen, and did exaggerated, cow-like social greetings: "M-O-O-O!" I determined that a cap signifying membership in this newly-initiated Bovine Birders Club was needed. The cap features a Holstein cow wearing a set of bright red binoculars around her neck. Appreciative Club members were truly M-O-O-V-E-D by the caps. My Portland surgeon was also an honorary cap recipient, and deservedly so.

Dump Picking

Although more than forty years have elapsed, I recall an experience at the former Bristol Town Dump, a genuine, old-fashioned trash dump in those days, with a proud tradition of dump picking. I'd parked next to a smartly-dressed lady in a gleaming, open-topped convertible. As I exited my rusting F-100 pickup, the lady and I focused on an item lying between us on the ground. It was a full-length raccoon coat in pristine condition! How I coveted that coat! But the lady had arrived mere seconds ahead of me, and, according to accepted dump-picking protocols, she held the technical *first dibs* on the coat. We stood there in awkward contemplation. Would this affluent woman claim an abandoned garment from the smelly turf of a public dump? She nervously struggled for the right words, before claiming the coat: "I'll just bet my daughter would wear that old coat to a college football game!" Defeated, I stepped back as she retrieved her furry prize.

Open dumps are mostly remnants of the past now, but it might surprise people that birders peruse large-scale city dumps, like the Hatch Hill Landfill in Augusta, on a regular basis. To a degree, Hatch Hill caters to birders, who must sign-in to gain admission. The birders must not physically enter the trash heaps, where mulling bulldozers and sanitation trucks are at work. I have visited the site, mounting a hillside overlook from Mt. Trashmore on the west side of the facility. From this open prominence, the grand scheme of modern society's waste volume is palpable, as tons of bagged trash cascade down its banksides.

Bald eagles and red-tailed hawks soar overhead or sit expectantly in the surrounding oaks. Crow and starling flocks circulate the property, and wintering song sparrows hide among the tall weeds. Hatch Hill has recorded some impressive bird sightings, particularly among its ranks of elite gulls that include glaucous and Iceland gulls, slaty-backed gull (northeastern Asia), and Thayer's gull, a species of high Arctic Canada that more typically winters along the U.S. West Coast.

The thought of the Thayer's gull spurred my curiosity. Though accorded full species status by the American Ornithological Union in the past, some had speculated whether Thayer's gull was a legitimate species unto itself, or simply a subspecies of the complex of Iceland gulls. Scientific research touches on such matters, as comparative DNA analyses and other factors help to establish precise classifications among closely-related species. A species is defined as a group of organisms capable of interbreeding and producing fertile offspring. And then there are the waterfowl, species such as mallards and black ducks that freely hybridize. Hybridizations can get tricky.

Through scientific analysis processes, new species are ordained when genetic evidence reveals chromosomal characteristics worthy of species status. This can result in previously singular species being "split" into two or more separate species. Birders who focus on keeping checklists grin broadly when new species are created, and groan when separate species are lumped together as one.

Standing on the dump precipice, my mind percolated. I pondered whether some formative new species, still unknown to science, was present. Had these familiar looking birds, sharing this isolating dump environment, been somehow transmuted into novel species? My imagination took over. Perhaps those cawing crows contained a few individuals of the dump-crow clan (*Corvus brachyrhynchos dumpus*). And those oddly-behaving herring gulls: I envisioned them with specialized bills, evolved with rows of serrated teeth for ripping open trash bags. Could these possibly be *Larus argentatus dumpasus?* Abruptly roused by a shrill backup beeper on the heavy equipment, I postponed these weighty matters for another day.

Just Ask Alexa

I admit to being a dinosaur when it comes to dealing with technology. I still wear an everyday wrist watch and carry a utilitarian cell phone strictly for functions of work duties or dire emergencies. I don't tweet, post on Instagram, or get social media updates on Facebook. I consult grandchildren for advice about routine techno protocols, such as setting a digital wristwatch. But suddenly, a new cloud-based voice assistant had entered my domain. My wife purchased an Amazon Echo, a black cylindrical device equipped with unending databases of computer-spawned information of practically any category. Alexa is the device's "spokesperson," a pleasant-enough sounding automated web robot (a "bot") available around the clock to answer queries about a constellation of subjects. Just give her a vocal prompt, and she will play your favorite music and adjust its volume to your proper liking.

Sensing my general disdain for Alexa, my wife urged me to ask her an occasional question, but I declined. To my delight, I soon detected some gaps in Alexa's musical compendium when she couldn't summon a particular song my wife had requested: "Sorry, I am not familiar with that song," she said. Wearing a gleeful smile, I smugly retorted, "Alexa, would it help you if we hummed a few bars?" Her feeble response: "I am not familiar with that request."

Just for kicks, I chose to ask her some bird-related questions. "Alexa, what is a bird?" She replied instantly with a quote from Wikipedia: "Birds are a group of endothermic vertebrates, characterized by feathers, toothless beaked jaws, the laying of hard-shelled eggs, a high metabolic rate, a four-chambered heart, and a strong yet lightweight skeleton."

If we unpack Alexa's canned response, there is relevant biological content inside. Unlike groups of reptiles and amphibians, birds are able to generate their own body heat internally. This ability is enhanced by their high metabolic rate and elevated body temperatures. Layers of insulating feathers help to preserve body heat levels. The highly-efficient heart is proportionally larger than mammal hearts, and it beats faster to supply oxygenated blood for flight and other physically demanding tasks.

The laying of hard-shelled eggs is a matter of practical necessity, since incubating birds must sit atop the eggs during incubation. In the 1970s, this literally became a serious issue for incubating raptors as the de-calcifying effects of DDT pesticide thinned and weakened egg shells to the point of widespread nest failures.

Bird flight is a demanding, but essential, life function that becomes accentuated during the takeoff and landing phases. The strong, lightweight skeletal structure of birds is composed of mainly thin and hollow bones that are specifically adapted for flight. Some bones even have pneumatic air sacs and do not contain marrow at all. Due to the weight contingencies of flight, birds have a smaller total number of bones than mammals and reptiles.

Next, I posed an open-ended question: "Alexa, can you tell me a bird fact?"

"Birds live on all seven continents," she offered.

Finally, I pressed her further: "Alexa, will snowy owls occur in Maine in the coming winter?"

"I'm not sure about that. I'm still learning more about birds," she explained.

I conceded that I have much more to learn about them, as well.

Making a List; Checking It Twice

Since we humans are the only species with list-keeping skills, this phenomenon is undoubtedly a unique capacity of the human brain. Typical lists serve as daily reminders of things needing our attention: the classic "to-do" lists. Lists can also confirm completed tasks, and set new goals for future accomplishments. That's basically how bird checklists function for most bird watchers: as a summary of species already seen, and a wish list of possible or desirable future sightings.

There are numerous possibilities for generating bird lists, depending on your personal preferences. Some birders keep a yearly checklist of species seen during one calendar year; others pare the list down to a monthly or weekly level. Tell-tale signs, indicating when a birder's interest is piqued by a specific sighting, include the familiar refrain: "I NEED that bird!" Other listing options include state and county lists. Some birders keep a yard list of birds seen at their feeders or the nearby vicinity. And ultimately, many birders maintain comprehensive lists of all species encountered throughout their lifetimes. These are the highly venerated life lists, testaments of dogged persistence and, in some cases, birding prowess. It should come as no surprise that, occasionally, life lists are brandished as bragging rights. But, in truth, a prodigious life list does not automatically confer expert knowledge of the birds in question. Like most worthwhile endeavors, that requires devoted time and effort.

Some life lists are kept in a treasured old notebook, on field trip cards, or in modern online databases, such as eBird. Media entities, such as eBird, provide immediate and historical access to individualized entries placed in the system (a cumulative, up-to-date bird list.) Through eBird's data-crunching power, regional range maps for specific species are available as well.

Several of my friends employ their favorite birding field guide as a record repository, noting the date and location of sightings next to the guide's illustrations. While some birders may forget to register their motor vehicle or their anniversary date, they can probably recall details of when and where they saw a vagrant warbler, hawk, or shorebird.

The practice of listing has its devotees and detractors. A high-caliber British birder once stated, "There is no serious birding without lists." Is that possibly true? My personal experience with checklists has run hot and cold through time. Today, I have no comprehensive list of total birds seen during my lifetime. Instead, I have remnants of local and regional bird lists generated through various time spans. During adolescence, I found that compiling checklists was worthwhile and satisfying, since I was constantly discovering new birds back then.

Some years ago, I began keeping an inclusive "state list" of birds I'd seen within Maine borders. I used a pre-printed card consisting of species that had occurred within the state. When that listing card eventually filled to near capacity, I penciled-in occasional rare or vagrant species not included on the card. When I ran out of space on the back of the card, I ceased making formal entrees altogether. And since I seldom chase rare bird sightings, I've undoubtedly passed on a considerable number of obvious rarities. On the other hand, I've also savored some memorable excursions with fellow birders when a sizzling "target bird" was the primary objective of the day.

I'll end with a hypothetical exercise in self-inquiry: If an ivory-billed woodpecker sighting were confirmed somewhere in the southern U.S., would I travel there to see it? It's unlikely. But there's a conditional proviso, as well—that's only if the legendary (and most likely extinct) species were verified somewhere north of Kittery.

Loon in a Bathtub

Throughout the summer months, the mournful yodels of the common loon epitomize the primal call of wilderness on Maine lakes and ponds. In fall, loons vacate inland locations and remote interior breeding sites of the upper U.S. and Canada to winter along the Atlantic seaboard. As adults relocate to the ocean, juveniles gather in fall flocks on northern lakes, awaiting their ocean sojourns in later weeks. The juveniles will remain on the ocean for the following two years. In the third year, those immature birds will return inland, but will not actually breed until they reach five to six years of age. Loons are generally long-lived creatures that can well afford to wait several years before launching into breeding activity. One particular, leg-banded female was recorded at over twenty-nine years old.

Two loon memories stand out for me. One frigid December morning, I discovered an evolving emergency at Rockland's Chickawaukee Lake, where two loons had become trapped by a rapid overnight freeze-up of the entire lake. A creeping ice sheet had formed in previous days, leaving only narrowing channels of open water at mid-lake. For a week, I'd noticed the two tardy loons diving in a hundred-yard stretch of open water. Loons are heavy-bodied birds that must patter and taxi across the water to achieve flight.

Now frigid overnight temperatures had sealed the lake, isolating the struggling pair to a narrow, twenty-foot trench of water. The birds maintained a slim crease in the vice-like ice by churning the water with their wings and feet and shrugging their shoulders against the sharp, icy edges. With no apparent means of escape or rescue, they appeared doomed. Life-ending freeze-ins of loons occur on occasion.

Later that day, temperatures warmed miraculously, and a warm, steady rain began to descend. When I returned to check, the ice sheet had dissipated to gaping open sectors. The freed loons had successfully escaped.

The second memory involves a loon spending a few hours in my bathtub. That's right, and I'm not talking about a rubber ducky toy loon. What led to this unusual circumstance? A local lobsterman reported a loon that had stranded itself on the shoreline at New Harbor. Since loons are extremely awkward on land and would normally go ashore only to nest, any landlubbing loon is typically a sick or injured bird.

We approached the helpless loon as it lay on the gravel beach above the tideline. It appeared lethargic and weak, and was likely dehydrated. Back in the 1980s, cell phones were unavailable, and quality wild bird rehab facilities, such as today's Avian Haven, were scarce. I'd brought along a thick bath towel to rap and secure the bird for safe transport to my house, where we would phone a Damariscotta veterinarian for advice and possible treatment of the bird.

Needless to say, the loon did not welcome our well-meaning aid, nipping our fingers and wriggling its feet and shoulders to escape. At home, I filled the bathtub with cold water to a depth of a foot or more and delicately placed the loon inside. Sensing the familiar cold water beneath it, the bird fanned out its immense webbed feet and began to relax a bit.

Interiors of home bathrooms are sometimes attributed with superlative acoustical qualities. And, truth be known, my meager operatic performances during morning showers sound relatively majestic (to me, at least) within the acoustical confines of the tub chamber. But I was not prepared, in the least, for the echoing loon serenade that soon transpired! The loon's tremulous, yodeling wails resonated so deeply that I sensed the reverberations through my chest walls. Despite this unlikely setting, the loon did precisely what loons were created to do: proclaim their sacred wildness from any random patch of water to anyone with ears to hear.

Mad About Decoys

In the late 1970s, I met a summer boater returning to New Harbor from an exploratory trip to Eastern Egg Rock, an island restoration site for Atlantic puffins in Muscongus Bay. The man was very excited as he announced that he'd just photographed a dozen puffins perched tamely atop the boulder-strewn shorelines of the island. In actuality, he had photographed the wooden puffin decoys placed there to recruit wild puffins back to their former nesting colonies on the Rock. A few years later, live Atlantic puffins would eventually re-inhabit the island. Starting with those initial decoys, the budding era of avian "social attraction" efforts had begun.

Pioneered through the ingenuity of Puffin Project founder Dr. Steve Kress, conservation decoys and, later on, sound-producing devices and mirror boxes became standard tools in modern global efforts to restore diminished or abandoned seabird sites. Researchers around the world have employed these methods to restore more than forty-five different seabird species through 120 separate restoration projects.

Through December 2016, the Mad River Company, a longtime Vermont canoe manufacturer, with a sideline in the decoy business, was a leading provider of conservation decoys. When the Mad River owners decided to retire, they donated their decoy-making equipment to Bremen's Audubon Hog Island Camp, home to the Puffin Project. The production equipment included molds for a variety of seabird species and two baking ovens required in the manufacturing process.

I toured the Mid-Coast Audubon decoy site (renamed as Mad River Decoys by Audubon) with Seabird Sue Schubel, who works on various aspects of seabird restoration projects. The factory barn's work benches and shelves spoke of creative energy: rows of finished plover, tern, and puffin decoys were mingled with an assortment of works in progress. Several outbound decoy shipments sat by the doorway. Along with Eric Snyder, the facilities manager of Hog Island Audubon Camp, this able team had manufactured and sold roughly four hundred decoys of thirty-six species, in its first year of operation.

Once the iron molds are filled with plastic polymer material, they are baked until hardened. Next, each decoy is cleaned up and painstakingly hand-painted with specific markings as to its species. The finished decoys are then individually bubble-wrapped and boxed for shipment.

Globally, seabird restoration measures encompass a range of species. Where are these decoys heading? How about common tern orders from New York, Michigan, Switzerland, and the Netherlands? Aleutian tern decoys are sent to Alaska; crested terns to Australia; least terns to Louisiana and Guadeloupe; snowy plovers to California. Black-footed and Laysan's albatross decoys are needed in Hawaii. The large, life-sized albatross decoys come in two different poses, one exhibiting a sky-pointing posture that is typical of adult breeding behavior.

Sue also produces an innovative line, Murremaid Music Boxes. These are solar-powered sound devices that play looping vocalizations to attract particular seabird species. Seabird colonies are noisy, highly acoustical environments, where vocal communication plays a supporting role in recruitment of new members. Nesting pairs also vocalize to proclaim territory and maintain auditory contact.

With a bit of whimsical artistic license, Sue has fashioned colorful fist-sized maracas in the pointy shapes of murre eggs. She calls these blue and speckled beauties "Murre-acas." Decoy production takes a summer break, but resumes in November.

Page-Turner

In March, 2020, I visited Bowdoin College's Special Collections Library to participate in its monthly page-turner event. Bowdoin is fortunate to possess a copy of John James Audubon's *The Birds of America*, which is on permanent display there. Printed between 1827 and 1838, it contains 435 life-size hand-colored engravings of North American birds, printed on handmade paper. The "double elephant–sized" folio measures 39.5 inches tall by 28.5 inches wide. Originally, the hand-engraved, unbound prints were issued in tin cases containing sets of five every month or two. With each delivery, a subscriber received images of one large bird, three small birds, and one medium-sized bird. The frenetic pace of Audubon's ambitious project kept him bouncing between acquiring and painting of new species of birds, combined with his alternate efforts to market the prints in Europe and North America. At a cost of around $1,000, *The Birds of America* had a limited list of purchasers consisting principally of wealthy patrons and institutions. Today only 120 copies are believed to exist—107 in institution collections and thirteen in private hands.

What are Bowdoin's page-turner events all about? On the first Friday of the month, the glass-shrouded folio case is rolled open, and two librarians delicately flip one giant page to the next. One might expect that white gloves are required for this process, but that's not the case. It seems that wearing of gloves diminishes the turners' sensitivity of touch when handling the priceless pages. Clean, freshly-washed hands are the best tools for the job.

Since 2016, these monthly events have drawn between forty-five and seventy visitors, including one who travels from Massachusetts. Directly following the page-turning event, a guest speaker describes each new species of the month and makes a few remarks to the audience. That's where I entered the picture. Named by Mr. Audubon himself, my page species was the "black and yellow wood-warbler." If that name doesn't ring familiar, there's a good reason. When Alexander Wilson, another early and famous ornithologist, shot and collected one of these warblers from a magnolia tree some years later, it was renamed as the magnolia warbler.

A spring magnolia warbler in vibrant breeding plumage is truly a sight to behold. With its black facial mask and distinctive black breast bands that radiate onto a deep-yellow chest, "maggies" nest in small conifers and forage low in the understory, picking insects from the undersides of leaves. Their energetic tail-flashing behavior helps to expose insects to capture.

In speaking on a theme of carrying forward Audubon's spirit of natural inquiry, I mentioned three of my contemporaries who contributed gains in our current understanding of birds and their conservation. These three were Mark Libby, a birder and commercial fisherman of New Harbor, whose decades of significant bird records documented the presence of rare, and not-so-rare, pelagic and land species. Ralph S. Palmer was a noted Maine ornithologist, who published *Maine Birds* in 1949. His unifying clarifications of the state's historical bird records provided a solid foundation for further bird study. Peter Vickery, a renowned birder and researcher with a keen interest in grassland species, worked to support grassland conservation work at Kennebunk Plains and other preserves. His long-awaited book, *The Birds of Maine*, was published posthumously.

And so, Bowdoin's successful page-turning events will continue for quite a spell. The progressive unveiling of Audubon's entire folio, at a rate of one species a month, will require thirty-six years to complete.

Personal Ads

"Refined, healthy, well-educated man, thirty-five years old, blue eyes, brown hair, weight 160, five-foot-nine, wishes to correspond with lady able to finance good business proposition. I am a construction engineer and know the business thoroughly; object, wedding bells and business success for both parties. Bank references given, and expected in return. All replies treated strictly confidential. Box 8, X4-Post."

Now that online dating services are so popular, the old-fashioned personal ads in newspapers and other publications are becoming passé. Those ads were often informative, humorous and quirky in nature, and definitely entertaining.

Of course, birds use more direct physical means for evaluating and choosing their potential mates. Practical considerations, such as singing talents, plumage features, and the quality of a prospective nesting territory, are fundamental to final mate selections. But what if birds could submit personal ads of their own? If they could, here's what they might say:

Turkey Vulture: Balding, mature gentleman who winters in New Jersey seeks female companion to cruise the summer skies. With my broad six-foot wingspan, I am a regal soaring machine. My current weight is a trim four pounds. I'm a diet-conscious individual who focuses mainly on low-fat entrees, but I can be very eclectic in what I choose to eat. Admittedly, I'm not much of a nest builder, but have been quite successful at rearing several offspring in hollow stumps, under boulders, and in caves.

Common Tern: Seasoned, continental traveler who inhabits realms of perpetual summer seeks like-minded counterpart. Not to boast, but I've been called rather elegant, and my agile, buoyant flight style is envied by many. For three summers, I've accompanied other terns to Maine's Eastern Egg Rock, where I revel in attacking and harassing the island biologists in my spare moments. I'm also a reliable provider and loyal nest mate, with proven nesting results to my credit. I'm residing in coastal Argentina this winter, and should arrive in Maine by mid-May. Come fly with me, baby!

Double-crested Cormorant: Would you like to meet a rangy, angular fellow with attractive turquoise-colored eyes and a glossy suit of black feathers? I am truly skilled at diving for fish, and enjoy spending my leisure time drying my wings on sunny ledges. Perhaps we could rendezvous during the spring alewife run on the Georges River in May. Have you ever been there? Fish are always so plentiful, but watch out for those hungry eagles. Perhaps I could keep a protective eye on you? By springtime, I'll be adorned with two shaggy head crests and looking at my best.

Black-crowned Night-Heron: If you are seeking a full, active nightlife, I'm your guy. Join me for picturesque dusks along riverbanks and moonlit marshes. I know many secluded, quiet places for fine evening dining. When I return to my nest grove along Thomaston Harbor in April, I hope to see YOU there. P. S. Please don't mind my ad photo too much. It's an early one, taken during my adolescence, long before I acquired my rakish gray-and-black feathers, not to mention my streaming white head plumes.

Perspectives

My friend John shared an experience that illustrates how personal perspectives can shape and drive our decision-making processes. After living outside the state for several years, John and his wife contemplated where they would permanently settle—perhaps build a house somewhere in Maine? Raised near the Pemaquid River in Bristol, John spent his boyhood fishing and exploring the local rivers. His wife grew up in a major, metropolitan area environment. One spring afternoon, the couple stood at the edge of the Pemaquid River to survey a potential wooded house lot. To punctuate the visit, for John at least, a fat trout broke the water surface, leaping airborne to devour an insect! "Wow!" thought John, "This is a definite sign that we should purchase this incredible property!" Meanwhile, his wife stood by silently. What were her thoughts? "Just get me out of this dismal, bug-infested wilderness!" Needless to say, they located elsewhere.

Today's world is full of conflicting perceptions on many fronts. And with competing political and social narratives in play these days, spheres of public opinion are increasingly fragmented, blurring the lines between legitimate facts and fiction.

Let's consider the effects of plastic waste products on the natural environment as a topic of public interest. Plastics that end up in ocean habitats have lasting consequences. In 1907, a Belgian inventor created the first plastic substances through synthesizing phenol and formaldehyde. In 1953, high-density polyethylene (No. 2 plastic) came into gradual use in plastic grocery bags. By the end of 1985, 75 percent of supermarkets were offering plastic bags. Since plastic products abound to serve modern society's needs, management and responsible disposal of these materials is now the crux of a deepening dilemma.

When you gaze out onto Atlantic waters, the ocean appears as a clean, limitless expanse, but satellite images reveal a different picture. Unfortunately, "one-time use" plastic items and other forms of hard plastics find their way into the world's ocean currents. Much of this ocean plastic waste accumulates in five swirling global ocean gyres (North and South Atlantic, North and South Pacific, and Indian Ocean). Technically, these immense trash vortexes (one is double the size of the state of Texas) are big enough to warrant a zip code address. Plastics constitute about 90 percent of these floating garbage patches.

This plaguing issue involves marine animals that ingest plastic debris, mistaking it for food. Sea turtles, seabirds, fish, and whales are species of greatest concern. One recent example was a thirty-one-foot sperm whale washed ashore on the Indian Ocean coastline. With thirteen pounds of plastic in its stomach, he carried around 115 plastic cups, 4 plastic bottles, twenty-five plastic bags, two flip-flops, a nylon sack, and one thousand other assorted pieces of plastic. Some plastics eventually break down, releasing chemical compounds that impact animals' ability to feed and reproduce. Despite futile attempts at large-scale clean ups, these gargantuan sites are rapidly expanding.

Are things any better as birds encounter plastics on the dry land? For folks who spend time observing birds, we routinely see remnants of plastic in nesting structures of ospreys and a wide variety of songbirds, such as robins and brown thrashers. After all, birds are mobile creatures with relatively large brains, capable of problem-solving and adapting to modest habitat changes. In urban settings, where natural building materials might be in shorter supply, birds often modify their nests with man-made materials. Strips of plastic bags, tinsel, paper, or aluminum foil may be substituted for leaves, mosses, and grasses. Ribbons of electrical cable, string, or rope may supplant a platform of traditional wooden nesting sticks. Are these resourceful birds lucky survivors of the era of plastics or thriving exploiters of their new normal?

Photographing That Bird

My earliest remembrance of a photo camera was the boxy Brownie Hawkeye owned by my mother. In the 1950s era, people mailed away their exposed rolls of film to be developed, or dropped them at the local pharmacy for shipment. Weeks later, we eagerly examined those routinely blurry images of our pets, kids at the beach, birthday parties, and family gatherings. Gluttons for punishment, we might even order double-copies of these same photos to share with others.

When I first began photographing birds as an adult, I took "digiscoped" photos by pairing my 30x spotting scope with a small hand-held digital camera. Focusing the scope precisely on a stationary bird, I'd merely center the camera lens inside the scope ring and press the camera shutter. This technique worked well enough with cooperative, still subjects, such as roosted shorebirds or gulls, but couldn't capture birds in flight.

My present camera rig, a Canon 7D Mark 2 with a 400mm fixed lens, permits decent flight photos and nicely-detailed close-ups much of the time. Under optimal lighting conditions, its eight-frames-per-second shutter can freeze flight images with clarity. The versatility of digital photography affords immediate feedback to review and edit images. This instructive review process can help to improve future results. In truth, I use the camera's Delete button a lot!

While I'm not a polished or trained photographer, I've acquired some practical photo knowledge through direct field experiences and novice experimentation. But much of what I've learned relates largely to the birds themselves and their behavior, rather than to super-honed camera techniques.

Getting close to birds when possible is a factor worth mentioning. Each species has a basic "comfort zone," a distance where the birds are tolerant of human approach without fleeing the scene. Species accustomed to people, such as gulls and rock pigeons, are invariably easier to approach and photograph. Blue-winged teals are often confident photo subjects, while their smaller cousins, the green-winged teal, are more likely to vacate during an approach. Discretion is required during nesting seasons, so as not to crowd birds or disrupt feeding or other critical life activities. Getting an amazing nest photo is not worth the price of disrupting the nest or, worse, causing an incubating parent to abandon the site.

How do we approach feathered subjects without causing them undue stress? Let the bird feel safe and natural during your approach. Move patiently and gradually, not rushing the scene. Take a few slow steps and pause. Instead of moving directly toward the bird, approaching from an oblique angle will generally get you closer to the subject.

For instinctive survival reasons, birds are acutely aware of animal and human predators observing them. Birds are experts at reading body language. They may feel threatened or suspicious if you stare directly at them or quickly raise and point binoculars and cameras in their direction. Often, I will feign disinterest, and may temporarily turn my back and nonchalantly face in the opposite direction.

Photo blinds are helpful, but you don't need to purchase a camo photo set-up. Being a natural cheapskate, I once draped an old bedsheet, complete with customized scissor peephole to accommodate the camera barrel, across some curtain rods at my "man cave" at home. Through that mystical window porthole, I've chronicled the social interactions of visiting eagles, hawks, ravens, and gulls competing for food scraps in the backyard. Your car interior may also serve as a suitable roadside photo blind—you might start a new trend of drive-up photography! Some of my best photos were obtained straight out the car window. In winter, however, waves of heat rising from the car's interior may result in somewhat wavy quality images.

Easy photo tips? Focus your lens on the eye of the bird. Regardless of how crisp or well composed an image might otherwise be, an out-of-focus eyeball will detract from the photo's overall quality. Best photo times are early morning or later in the afternoon—the "golden light" times of day when birds are also likely to be active.

Scarce as Hen's Teeth

The other day I watched a herring gull swallow an entire twelve-inch fish in one gulp. Being hotly pursued by a second gull, the first bird swallowed the fish to avoid imminent robbery. In order to maintain high metabolic rates and elevated body temperatures (101 to 112 degrees Fahrenheit), birds must consume more food in proportion to their size than most other animals. Their digestive processes are impressively efficient in this regard. A barred owl typically digests a meal in about ninety minutes; in thirty to forty minutes, black ducks digest and pass blue mussels through their digestive tracts. Processing meals of watery berries in sixteen to forty minutes, cedar waxwings are possible champions of rapid digestion.

While they don't chew their food as toothed creatures do, birds have a formidable capacity to digest complex diets. The intake process is driven by the particular bill size and shape to handle certain food types. Whether it's the flesh-tearing beaks of raptors, uniquely fashioned insect and seed-eating bills, or highly specialized bills of hummingbirds, food is initially prepared for digestion inside the bill.

Lacking teeth, birds have a muscular gizzard that grinds and mashes hard-textured foods into more digestible bits. The gizzards of wood ducks and wild turkeys, for example, can readily crush whole acorns, a dietary staple. The gizzard's powerful grinding action is further enhanced by abrasive elements of grit, gravel, and even small stones that are consistently ingested with food.

The bird's crop is an enlargement of the upper esophagus that serves as a temporary food storage organ. This allows hawks, owls, and vultures that may go hungry for hours or days to gorge on large quantities when food opportunities arise. Comprised of undigested scraps of fur, feathers, bones, bills, claws, and teeth of small mammals, intestinal pellets are regurgitated on a regular basis. Deposited on the ground beneath steady roosting sites, pellets vary in shape, from spherical, to oblong to plug-like. Flycatchers, and even plant-eating birds, expel pelletized exoskeletons of insects and indigestible plant matter.

Birds with crops fill their stomach about twice a day, while insect-eating birds average five to six times a day. I observed a mourning dove gobbling down nearly two hundred sunflower seeds in a single feeding session, its swelling crop expanding proportionally.

Some quirky digestive habits? Members of the grebe family routinely ingest quantities of feathers and feed feathers to their young. It is speculated that ingested feathers function as a strainer between the stomach and small intestine, and may help birds retain fish bones in the stomach long enough for fuller digestion. And the subsequent formation and movement of pellets back through the upper digestive column may cleanse the esophagus of intestinal parasites.

Maine summer residents, black-billed cuckoos demonstrate yet another odd but practical digestive scheme. Feeding on a primary diet of caterpillars and fall webworms, these neo-tropical birds accumulate mats of fuzzy, stiff spines in their stomachs. When the spines accumulate to the point of clogging discomfort, the cuckoos periodically shed their stomach lining. Cuckoos are also observed to bang caterpillars against branches, possibly to remove some spines before ingestion.

Skepticisms

A degree of optimism can be a useful quality when aiming to identify birds. After all, without some optimistic prospect of success, why would anyone have the courage to even begin? I recall a field trip where a non-birding spouse had accompanied his birder wife, just for the experience. As our group scanned a swampy wooded section, the husband unwittingly announced the highlight species of the day with an honest inquiry: "What's that little owl over there?" The novice then pointed out a skulking saw-whet owl peering at us inside a tree cavity!

Whether for novices or seasoned birders, the bird identification process is really a blend of art and science and, sometimes, plain dumb luck. But the power of suggestion also makes any field guide a double-edged sword. Occasionally, thorny issues of ID skepticisms arise, creating uncertainty among birders. In a best-case scenario, however, those puzzling or confusing IDs should serve as constructive opportunities that lead to deeper knowledge of a species by all parties concerned. But, let's face it. Anyone who does lots of birding will periodically make missed calls. This includes birders at considerably high skill levels. Redemption comes if or when they freely recognize the error and revisit their first impressions. That's how we all learn and improve our birding skills.

Reports of rare birds that were initially misidentified or delayed abound. In January 1975, two members of the Brookline (Massachusetts) Bird Club stood fifty feet from a Ross's gull, a smallish pink-breasted gull that was previously unrecorded south of Alaska. Not expecting this vagrant species in Newburyport, the pair was stumped at first. Paging through field guides that evening, they eventually concluded it was certainly a Ross' gull. Next they phoned a representative of the local birding hotline, who wrote down the information but, not believing them, declined a hotline posting. Other nearby birders showed little interest in pursuing such an "unrealistic" sighting.

On March 2, six weeks later, the gull reappeared—this time on the *CBS Evening News;* its image had also found its way into *Time* magazine. Through the entire hubbub, the two men who initially reported the bird were generally unmentioned and forgotten.

But it gets worse. Back on December 28, 1974, a man named James Nash had also observed the gull at the Newburyport mudflats. At that earlier date, its breast color was a bright pink, far pinker than that of the March sighting. "The possibility that it was a Ross' hit me pretty quickly," he later wrote, "but I was all alone, and I'd never heard of anyone reporting a Ross' gull, and no other birdwatchers were around to verify it with me." That night when he arrived home, he told his wife, "I just saw something that couldn't be what it was." Nash added, "She and my children wanted me to report it, but I didn't want to be taken for a fool."

Nash mentioned the sighting to a non-birding friend at work. Two months later in the office hallway, the friend told him, "That thing you saw at Newburyport has been confirmed." "What are you talking about?" Nash asked. "That Ross' gull. It was on television last night."

We might recall the vagrant great black hawk seen in Biddeford and Portland in 2018. The original discovery was made by a curious lady who photographed the "strange-looking" hawk, and posted her sighting on Facebook. Her simple query: "What is this bird?" As more people studied her posting, speculation about a possible great black hawk began to emerge. Soon thereafter, the errant tropical hawk's true identity was confirmed. But, even then, there were temporary suspicions that the bird in question had been Photo-shopped into a green background of Maine foliage. Subsequent live sightings quickly dispelled that rumor though. The take-away measure here: in nature, we can expect the unexpected.

Going to the Movies

In 2011, I went to see *The Big Year*, a movie about three zealous birders who set out on a 1998 competitive quest to find every conceivable bird species within North America, and try to break the then-existing continental record of 721 species observed in a single calendar year. Anyone with serious hopes of winning such a competition would need to cover diverse habitats from extreme northern Canada to Florida, the Texas/Mexico border, and the rugged, remote terrain of Attu Island at the tip of the Aleutian peninsular.

Approximately 675 bird species live in North America. In rough terms, about 440 of these live on land, 190 are found along shorelines, and 45 are pelagic species found well offshore. In order to reach the magical 700 zone, birders would need to "twitch" a fair number of out-of-range vagrants. Success would demand competent birding skills and a hefty measure of good luck and precise timing. By way of a localized comparison, my cumulative total for the Maine region was 326 species back in 2011. Since about 212 species nest in Maine, about one hundred of my remaining sightings consisted of seasonal migrants and a few rare vagrants.

I enjoyed the movie, although it probably won't be nominated for an Academy Award. The movie's producer had neglected to equip these globe-trotting birders with spotting scopes, an essential tool for the real-life participants. But the film provided insights into human nature, and highlighted the practical strategies and head games utilized to gain psychological advantages over their birding rivals.

By chance, I met up with one of *The Big Year*'s three actual participants, Greg Miller, at the 2006 American Birding Association National Convention held in Bangor. On several early mornings, we paired up and ventured to nearby birding locales. Greg was an amiable Ohio fellow with a reliable ear for bird song, and a penchant for stops at fast-food restaurants.

Of the movie's three Big Year birders, I identified most closely with Greg. He was an average working guy, who somehow managed to hold down a full-time job and carve out enough free time to traipse across the continent. By working long stints at the office, up to ninety hours, some weeks, he adjusted his job schedule as a data specialist. Even with Greg's amazing year-end total of 715 species, he finished third in the competition.

Obviously, this type of *Big Year* event is not suited for most of us. For many Maine birders, though, the enjoyment of finding and counting birds can be played out in different ways. Occasionally, I've done a Big Day circuit of coastal haunts as part of Audubon fundraising events. One late May, I tallied 130 coastal species in a single day. Slightly higher tallies are possible in sections of southern Maine, where a few more species nest.

Another variation on this theme are Big Sit events, where birds are tallied from a stationary location, one carefully chosen for its combined high-quality bird habitats and ample views of open sky. Some sit events span a twenty-four hour period, with teams of birders taking turns to monitor the site. Perhaps one of these Big Day options will appeal to you.

E is for Egg

Although eggs are found throughout the animal kingdom, egg-laying and terrestrial nest building are essential to avian reproduction. And since birds are aerial creatures, the females couldn't possibly fly around with those weighty eggs onboard. Could you picture a bomber-loaded female American robin cruising your neighborhood, burdened with an unhatched clutch of eggs?

Next time you crack an egg, check out its basic design. Inside the blunt end of the eggshell, you may notice a thin membrane that serves as a temporary air pocket. This slender air space comes into play at hatching time, providing the struggling hatchling with its first breath of air before launching the active hatching process. The chick then uses its egg-tooth (a small, hard nub on the tip of the upper mandible) to poke a rough hole through the shell casing and gradually divide the shell into two separate pieces.

The eggs of wild birds show a wide range of individualized, spherical shapes. Pyriform, or pear-shaped eggs with pointy ends, are typically laid by seabirds that nest on narrow edges of rocky sea cliffs. If somehow dislodged, these eggs are more likely to roll in a circle rather than tumbling straight over the edge.

While the calcium bicarbonate surface of birds' egg is inherently white, eggs come in assorted colors and complex spotted, splotched, and scrawled patterns. Birds nesting on exposed open ground, such as killdeer and piping plover, rely on cryptically-marked shell patterns that minimize detection by predators. Eggs of cavity nesters, like woodpeckers and kingfishers, are a plain white color. Inside the darkened nest cavity, egg color and pattern are less vital factors against detection.

Two basic egg-laying schemes create divergent outcomes for the hatchlings. Altricial eggs are laid by many types of songbirds. These eggs produce pin-feathered chicks that are essentially blind and dependent on parental care and feeding for about three weeks. Some altricial species, such as robins, produce two broods during the nesting season. By contrast, precocial eggs yield downy chicks that are relatively well developed and highly mobile shortly after hatching. Ruffed grouse, waterfowl, and shorebirds are examples of this approach.

A majority of species produce fixed or determinant numbers of eggs per clutch. Domestic hens, however, are indeterminate layers, meaning they can replace a lost egg by laying another. Female brown-headed cowbirds are a brood parasite that deposits eggs in host nests. With extraordinary egg-producing capabilities, cowbirds average nearly one egg per day for up to forty to seventy days. Their "lay and leave" strategy apparently works, since over 140 host species are documented as raising cowbird chicks.

Commercially-produced eggs are marketed as a nutritious component of dietary cuisines. This fact also led to widespread harvesting of seabird eggs at Maine's summer nesting colonies in the late nineteenth century. "Eggers" followed a prescribed protocol of breaking all eggs that were initially found. This practice ensured the freshness of any subsequent eggs gathered at these sites. Needless to say, the cumulative impact of egg-collection led to eventual collapse of most coastal nesting populations. In recent decades, seabird restoration projects under the auspices of the National Audubon Society and the Maine Coastal Islands National Wildlife Refuge have reversed some declines, but more needs to be done.

Birds' eggs are prized by any number of natural predators, including crows and ravens, raccoons, foxes, squirrels, and snakes. Red squirrels are especially efficient at foraging bird nests as they roam and explore forested settings. It is notable that species of snakes that specialize in egg predation have greatly reduced venom, inferring that the main function of venom is to subdue live prey. Of the nine species and two sub-species of Maine snakes, none is considered venomous.

Through the Eyes of Birds

It has been said of humanity that our eyes are the windows into the soul. Without question, our eyes can express an array of moods and emotions. When people fake a smile, though, onlookers can often tell, because the corners of the smiler's eyes do not crinkle up as they should. Birds have no concerns for smiling, but their large, powerful eyes are essential to their success and survival.

Vision is the most vital sensory system for birds. As such, avian visual acuity is estimated to be two to eight times better than that of humans. In relative-size comparisons with human skulls, birds' eyes are huge. Eyes of eagle's and the larger owl species are approximately people-sized. Ostrich eyeballs, with their longish, curled eyelashes, are nearly double the size of our own. Birds' outsized eyes are fixed inside the sockets, meaning that they must rotate their heads to peer behind or glance skyward.

The positioning of birds' eyes reveals much about their status as either a prey or predator species. The eyes of sparrows are located on the sides of the head, giving them a wide, peripheral field of view for detecting predators. In contrast, the eyes of predators are positioned closer to the front of the head, affording binocular vision and increased depth-perception while hunting.

Research has shown a unique neurological configuration that allows a state of vigilant "unihemispheric, slow-wave sleep," meaning that certain species can sleep with one eye open and one eye shut. Other visual advantages of birds include ability to view light within the ultra-violet spectrum and, and in many species, superior night-vision capabilities. The two eyelids function oppositely in various species: owls shut and blink their eyes by moving the top eyelid down (as we do); other birds elevate the bottom lid up to close the eye.

As with your cat or dog, birds also have a third eyelid called the *nictitating membrane*, a thin semi-transparent eyelid that sweeps horizontally across the eye surface to protect it from injury or to remove debris. Some raptors use the eyelid to protect their eyes while feeding their lunging nestlings. Cormorants and some diving birds have a transparent, centralized window in the nictitating eyelid that adjusts or corrects their underwater vision.

Focusing mainly on plumage details of birds, we may neglect to notice their eye color. The majority of birds have brown-toned eyes, but shades of color run the optical gamut. In some species, eye color evolves as the birds mature: the "baby-blue" eyes of young crows and ravens turn dark brown in adulthood. The eye color of woodland hawks, such as Cooper's and sharp-shinned hawks, transitions from light yellow to a deep reddish-orange as the hawks mature. And the naming of certain species, like red-eyed and white-eyed vireos, comes directly from their distinctive eye colors.

The actual color of bird's eyes is due to pigments, but, like bird feathers, apparent changes in coloration can result from refracted light conditions. Did you realize that the eyes of double-crested cormorants are a majestic deep turquoise? Did you know that the yellow eyes of snowy owls are of an almond-shape to reduce glare from Arctic ice and snow cover?

Yearbooks

Recently I browsed a copy of my old high-school yearbook. I was reminded of the passage of decades, the then-youthful faces in those senior class portraits. As the yearbook student editor, I had considerable input with the final product. By today's modern, high-tech standards, the 1965 *Bristolite* was an unsophisticated, amateurish volume, featuring Polaroid images (some overly-exposed) taken mainly in the school's gym. What I recall most, though, was the deep interpersonal connections made within this small-town school of about 120 students, where everyone actually knew their fellow students and teachers well. In fact, we knew each other well enough to nominate fellow students in fundamental character categories ranging from serious to silly: Most Likely to Succeed; Most Studious; Most Athletic; Best Buddies; Best Personality.

But what would a similar yearbook of Maine birds look like? Who might be selected Most Likely to Succeed? I would probably vote for the European starling. Back in 1890, sixty starlings were released in New York's Central Park as part of a literary scheme to introduce all of the birds mentioned in Shakespeare's sonnets to U.S. soil. With a current population numbering over 150 million individuals, the starling now extends from Alaska to Central America.

What lies behind their prodigious success story? Starlings are generalists, meaning they can adapt to broad dietary regimens across a range of habitats. In other words, starlings aren't picky about what they eat or where they live. Starlings increase their odds for nesting success by seeking out secure nesting cavities and then over-stuffing them with insulating materials to protect their nestlings.

Now back to the voting. Who might qualify for Most Athletic? If we consider powered swiftness and agility in the air, the peregrine falcon might fit the bill. If sustained flight capacity were a determining factor, I would nominate the Hudsonian godwit. Prior to their arrival on the Thomaston Harbor mudflats in fall, juvenile godwits have already flown two thousand miles from Arctic rearing tundra. The bulk of the adult godwit population simply overflies the entire North American continent on a four thousand-mile non-stop fall venture to southern South America.

Let's consider the Best Buddies category. Here I would favor the gregarious, highly social cedar waxwings. As nesting season concludes, waxwings form wandering flocks that scavenge for available fruits and berries. Altruism is an uncommon trait in nature. But, if you survey a waxwing flock stripping an apple or cherry tree in winter, observe them carefully. You may witness fruit being passed along, bill to bill, through a succession of flock mates. To me, this cooperative, communal behavior takes the category.

And finally, who wins the Best Personality award? Do birds and animals really possess discernable personality traits, you ask? Please inquire of any devoted dog or cat owner about their pet's adorable personality and endearing habits, and then get back to me.

If any bird epitomizes a pleasing personality style, I hereby nominate the perky black-capped chickadee. Adjectives such as cute, energetic, and approachable obviously apply to these hyperactive little fellows. If you feed birds at home, you will undoubtedly have your own chickadee encounters and memories to share.

Your Own Birding Patch

The terms "bird-watcher" and "birder" have slightly different connotations but are equally valid means of seeing and learning about birds through slightly different approaches. One pundit concluded that "bird-watchers" look at birds, while "birders" actively look for them. Competitive cross-country birding ventures grew more prevalent in the 1970s as people planned birding vacations involving hundreds or even thousands of travel miles. Despite criticisms of contributing to the globe's "carbon footprint," eco-travel conveys economic benefits to regions that are visited. Remember that vagrant great black hawk in Portland through December 2018? Visiting birders from all quarters added significantly to the city's coffers for those few special weeks. In some cases, nature tourism has moved the economic needle in tropical regions facing threats from broad-scale deforestation. Once a region's natural collateral attains a superior ecological value, its economic status and habitat preservation standards rise as well.

Thinking closer to home: Do you have a birding patch? This is an area that you bird frequently and know well. Familiarity affords obvious opportunities for increased knowledge of bird behavior and seasonal baselines of birds in your area. There are no formalized criteria for designating a yard or neighborhood as birding patch sector, just some general, guiding principles of understanding. Patch sizes can vary from a backyard or small neighborhood to transects of several square miles. Some patch boundaries are defined by fixed property lines or naturally occurring breaks in habitat. All birds seen (or heard) are fair game to record; fly-overs are countable, as well. Secondhand reports of birds by others are considered as off-limits. But you get to set the final rules for your own patch.

Guess what? I didn't realize until recently, but a rectangular, three-mile-long stretch of land I've birded with regularity for many years fits the definition of a birding patch! My particular patch is bordered by the Dragon Cement property on Route 1 in Thomaston, the upper sections of Weskeag Marsh on Buttermilk Lane, and the productive, lush hayfields in the vicinity of the Finnish Church on the Port Clyde Road.

My patch has delivered some memorable sightings in its day. Passing the Dragon plant property, I notice dark bird silhouettes atop the tall towers: peregrine falcons. Falcons take advantage of these lofty perches to rest, scan for prey, and possibly rear young. And, sure enough, a falcon pair has nested amid the plant's roof complexes, where three hatchlings were reported.

Peregrines really come to life at nearby Weskeag Marsh, with its rich availability of aerial prey. There I've witnessed stunning tail-chasing episodes, as streaking falcons pursued shorebirds and waterfowl. On one occasion, I stood riveted at mid-marsh as a scrambling blue-winged teal and a tail-riding peregrine rocketed straight at me. The grass-whizzing pair sailed within yards of each other, before the harried duck baled into the salt pannes, averting capture by mere inches.

Over several decades, Weskeag has rewarded me with thirty-one species of shorebirds. Most of the spring and fall migrants are the anticipated species that nest somewhere on the vast northern tundra. Rarer species, like a ruff from Eurasia and vagrant black-necked stilt, made cameo appearances there, as well. According to eBird data, Weskeag has hosted 210 species of birds at various times. And the summer hayfields along Route 131 pay special dividends of nesting bobolinks and eastern meadowlarks. Yes, this diverse patch of land has treated me very well!

PART VI

Some People Worth Knowing

My Friend Mark

"Friendship isn't a big thing—it's a lot of little things."

—Author Unknown

Before his death at age eighty-six, I spent nearly four decades birding throughout New England and eastern Canada with my good friend Mark Libby. He was a great birder and naturalist, who started birding as a kid growing up in Waterville. In the wee hours before school, Mark and several companions would ride their bicycles around town, studying the neighborhood birds and animals.

One morning Mark discovered a belted kingfisher nest tunnel inside the slope of a steep gravel pit. He scaled the banking and thrust his arm into the deep burrow. An adult kingfisher promptly latched onto his finger with its stout bill, sending Mark catapulting down the banking! Lesson learned. In the 1940s, Mark reported a nesting loggerhead shrike in Waterville, a seriously declining species that no longer nests anywhere near Maine.

After serving in the Navy in World War II, Mark decided not to return to college. Instead, he worked as a commercial fisherman out of New Harbor for fifty years. When asked why he chose fishing, Mark replied, "It was the only way I could think of to make a living and watch birds." In the early years of Mark's fishing career, comprehensive knowledge of seabird populations and their distributions was rudimentary, but Mark changed that.

Mark didn't post his sightings, and he never owned a computer. Rather, he kept precise handwritten notes on the seabirds and land birds he saw. He always carried a short pencil and a notebook in a chest pocket: "The faintest pencil is better than the sharpest mind," he would say.

Mark's handwritten notebooks go back to at least 1960, when he encountered, in the waters southeast of Monhegan Island, an adult yellow-nosed albatross, a great rarity in New England and North America waters. According to Mark, the giant seabird landed near his small dragger as he hauled back his net. Mark chopped up some fish and threw them to the hungry albatross, as he carefully sketched the bird in his notebook. In 1964, Mark recorded a second albatross.

Mark reported other unusual seabirds—pomarine jaegers and Manx shearwaters, and stray terns from farther south. Atlantic puffins, razorbills, murres. He knew these species well, and recorded them all in their seasonal cycles.

To birders familiar with Mark's considerable birding skills, he was often viewed as a "bird magnet," a guy who would consistently spot the odd or out-of-range species. In 1999, at Weskeag Marsh, he observed a drake garganey teal, an extremely rare Eurasian duck.

One August, Mark and I happened upon a storm-battered juvenile royal tern at Popham Beach. The dead tern wore a metal leg band that identified where and when it was banded. Mark learned that his longtime friend John Weske had banded the bird in North Carolina a month earlier. Separated by several hundred miles, the two friends had held the same bird!

Mark knew shorebirds thoroughly. His patient, methodic approach yielded curlew sandpipers and other rarities on numerous occasions. Once, at Weskeag Marsh, we were both surprised as a ruff, a rare Eurasian species, landed unexpectedly at our feet. We stood there motionless, watching the vagrant sandpiper foraging a few yards away. I whispered to him: "You know what that bird is, don't you?"

"Yup," he quietly answered.

In his modest, competent way, Mark added substantially to our knowledge and understanding of Maine birds. He also left an indelible impression upon my life.

Tom Martin and Monhegan Island

For six decades, expectant birders debarking from the Laura B ferry at the Monhegan harbor dock uttered a common refrain: "I wonder what's in Tom's yard?" They referred to Tom Martin, a lively, bigger-than-life New York City fellow who spent about a month on the island each spring and fall.

Over fifty years, Tom became the unofficial grandfather of birding on Monhegan. His narrow-framed yard was generously scattered with bird seed and halved oranges stacked on rugosa bush tops to welcome spring-arriving Baltimore and orchard orioles. He was a master film photographer who set up photo blinds on the harbor side premises. In all, Tom provided twenty-seven bird photographic plates for the three-volume set *The Audubon Master Guide to Birding*. In real ways, he alerted the birding public to the many rare sightings that have since graced Monhegan. His definitive photos of clay-colored sparrows and assorted out-of-range species came as a revelation to folks that had previously questioned his unusual reports. Along with Peter Vickery and iconic Maine ornithologist Ralph Palmer, Tom initiated the first Monhegan Christmas Bird Count in 1978.

He was a pioneering developer of macro-photographic techniques as well, capturing intriguing images of the delicate inner structures of flowers and wild grains. Tom was also a lifelong student of wild mushrooms and the assorted island plants.

Working as a highly skilled tool-and-die maker in his younger years, Tom had made it clear to his city boss that he would definitely need time off each May and September for extended stays on Monhegan. Tom added that, if this arrangement was not possible, he would simply have to seek a different job! Thankfully for us, his boss responded favorably.

When Tom passed at age ninety-four in December 2016, he left a legacy of deep friendships and generous hospitality to those who ventured into his island domain. Sharing knowledge of nature was his true life passion. Tom recounted a time once in Manhattan, when he sat on park bench and noticed a yellow-bellied sapsucker that had landed on a nearby tree trunk. Turning toward the lady seated next to him in his friendly, outgoing manner, he pointed at the tree and exclaimed, "Sapsucker!"

The lady replied, "Get away from me, you pervert!"

Tom's ashes are scattered on Monhegan. He is now back at the place he loved and where he belongs.

About the Author

Don Reimer is a lifelong birder and photographer residing in Warren, Maine. A board member of the Midcoast Audubon Society, he has led field excursions for local environmental organizations and the American Birding Association National Convention. He is a board member of the Friends of Maine Coastal Islands National Wildlife Refuge in Rockland, Maine.

Don has participated in multiple citizen/science projects, including Project Feeder Watch, the *Atlas of Breeding Birds in Maine* (1978–83), the Maine Owl Survey, and the International Shorebird Survey. He has served as compiler for the Thomaston–Rockland and Pemaquid–Damariscotta Christmas Bird Counts. Currently he serves as a regional coordinator for the 2018–22 *Maine Bird Atlas* project. His bimonthly column Birding with Don Reimer has appeared in the Rockland *Free Press* since 2007.